THE LAST J

MAIJU
LASSILA

THE LAST DAYS OF
MAIJU
LASSILA

A MEMOIR-NOVEL ABOUT THE WHITE TERROR FOLLOWING THE FINNISH CIVIL WAR

J.I. VATANEN

A PSEUDOTRANSLATION
BY DOUGLAS ROBINSON

atmosphere press

CONTENTS

TRANSLATOR'S PREFACE

Maiju Lassila was the most productive and most popular of the heteronyms created and deployed by the prolific Finnish novelist and journalist Algot Untola (1868-1918), who never published a single line under his own name. J I Vatanen was arguably the least productive and least popular of those heteronyms. Since this novel is presented as J I Vatanen's memoir of Maiju Lassila, one might be tempted to assume that the novel was actually written by Untola. The only problem with that would be that this memoir-novel was incontrovertibly written *after* Untola was summarily executed as a Red agitator by the triumphant White Army on May 21, 1918, one week after the Whites won the three-month Finnish Civil War—and the novel revolves around that execution and the White Terror of which it was an early exemplar. The detail with which Untola's demise is depicted in "The Pivot" (p. 109) and Chapter 7 of "After" provides circumstantial but pretty convincing internal evidence that Untola did not write it before his death. How could he possibly have predicted that he would be not just arrested, not just sentenced to death, not just executed, but thrown in the water off the transport ship and *then* shot to pieces in the water?

And in fact nobody knows who actually wrote the novel. The manuscript itself lies untyped, unpublished, unclaimed, and mislabeled in the Algot Untola/Maiju Lassila archive at the

National Library of Finland, marked in pencil as written/ finished in 1922. Conclusive evidence may some day turn up proving that it was in fact written pseudonymously by, say, Jalmari Finne (1874-1938) or Arvid Järnefelt (1861-1932); until such a day, we have to take a lot of this on faith.

So what is a heteronym? Are Maiju Lassila and J I Vatanen not actually Untola's *pseudonyms*?

It's complicated.

The term "heteronym" was coined by Fernando Pessoa (1889-1935), who famously had dozens of them—by some counts well over a hundred—notably Álvaro de Campos, who also figures as an amnesiac living in Guanajuato, Mexico, in Jim Gauer's 2016 *Novel Explosives*; Ricardo Reis, whose return to Portugal after Pessoa's death in 1935 became the premise of José Saramago's 1984 novel *The Year of the Death of Ricardo Reis*; and Alberto Caeiro, who was supposedly the teacher of the heteronym "Fernando Pessoa."[1] Though Pessoa coined the term "heteronym," however, the idea wasn't original with him; Søren Kierkegaard's experiments with anonymity and pseudonymity often veered into the territory that Pessoa called heteronymity. For example, in a postscript to his *Concluding Unscientific Postscript* (whose official author was the pseudoheteronym Johannes Climacus), he wrote:

> In *Either/Or*, I am just as little, precisely just as little, the editor Victor Eremita as I am the Seducer or the

---

[1] Four of Pessoa's heteronyms (Claude Pasteur, Vicente Guedes, Charles James Search, and Navas) were translators; Navas was the Portuguese translator of another of his heteronyms, an English fiction-writer and essayist named Horace James Faber. Some readers of this book may wonder whether the (pseudo)translator "Douglas Robinson" was not actually another of Algot Untola's infamous heteronyms. [Tr.]

Judge. He is a poetically actual subjective thinker who is found again in "In Vino Veritas." In *Fear and Trembling*, I am just as little, precisely just as little, Johannes de Silentio as the knight of faith he depicts, and in turn just as little the author of the preface to the book, which is the individuality-lines of a poetically actual subjective thinker. In the story of suffering ("'Guilty?'/ 'Not Guilty'"), I am just as remote from being Quidam of the imaginary construction as from being the imaginative constructor, just as remote, since the imaginative constructor is a poetically actual subjective thinker and what is imaginatively constructed is his psychologically consistent production.

In Pessoa's conception, too, a heteronym is not just a penname; it is an authorial persona with a fully fleshed-out biography and style. Ricardo Reis (b. 1887, and according to Saramago d. 1936) was a pagan Stoic neoclassicist and symbolist poet and a monarchist physician who fled Portugal to Brazil in 1919, after the monarchist rebellion was crushed; Alberto Caeiro (1889-1915) was a poor country boy who died young, but his philosophical poetry wielded a strong influence on both Ricardo Reis and Pessoa's heteronym "Fernando Pessoa"; Álvaro de Campos (b. 1890) was a decadent drunken futurist influenced by Walt Whitman who returned to Lisbon from London in 1926, the year the National Dictatorship was founded. And so on. All of his heteronyms were roughly his contemporaries—he was born in 1889—and male. For Pessoa these were not just pennames but multiple personalities. They emerged in his consciousness and started writing poems.

It occurs to me, too, thinking of "Fernando Pessoa" as one of Fernando Pessoa's heteronyms, that there is a "Douglas Robinson" heteronym in my 2020 transcreation of Volter Kilpi's *Gulliver's Voyage to Phantomimia*. As the "author" of that book Douglas Robinson translated Kilpi's unfinished Finnish novel into Swiftian English, wrote the continuation of that novel, still in that pastiche of Swiftian English, to the happy ending that Kilpi had planned for it, and created the paratextual frame for the novel, including not only the anonymous "random notes toward a vorticist manifesto," the "reader's report" by the fictional "Julius Nyrkki," and the "publisher's note" by Ethel Cartwright, but the "editor's introduction" by a somewhat confused and not-half-paranoid "Douglas Robinson." The ostensible *editor* of that book, who supposedly found the "original" English manuscript by Gulliver or Swift or whomever that the Kilpi-heteronym had supposedly "translated" into Finnish, was a Robinson-heteronym.[2]

In Algot Untola's case things look a little different, but just as complicated. For one thing, Untola has often been discussed under the (female) name Maiju Lassila. When Carl von Wendt, director of the Viapori/Suomenlinna prison camp to which Untola was being transported for execution, reported the successful completion of that execution to Senator Oswald Kairamo, he specifically said that they had shot Maiju Lassila. Articles and books about Untola since his death have often called him Maiju Lassila as well:

- The 1957 doctoral dissertation on Untola by Elsa Erho is titled "Maiju Lassila: Kirjallishistoriallinen tutkimus" ("Maiju Lassila: A Literary-Historical Study").
- Two years later, a 1959 radio profile of Untola by Unto Mietinen is titled "Maiju Lassilan jäljillä"

---

[2] This seems a bit self-aggrandizing for a translator's preface; could we at least bump this paragraph down to a footnote, or possibly even cut it altogether? [Ed.]

That reminds me: is "Douglas Robinson" the translator of this book not also a heteronym of "Douglas Robinson" the pseudotranslator? [Tr.]

("Tracking Maiju Lassila"), and a 2013 Web reposting of that profile by Juhana Säilynoja is titled "Mikä oli miehiään Maiju Lassila?" ("What Kind of a Man was Maiju Lassila?": https://yle.fi /aihe/artikkeli/ 2013/12/16/mika-oli-miehiaan-maiju-lassila).

- Leo Lindsten's 1977 biography of Untola is titled Maiju Lassila: Legenda jo eläessään ("Maiju Lassila: A Legend Even in Life").

- In the title of Eeva-Kaarina Kolsi's tabloid article on Untola, posted on the Web July 15, 2018, we are told that "Kirjailija Maiju Lassilan elämästä tuli karmea tragedia, kun rakastettu heitti hänen päälleen rikkihappoa" ("Writer Maiju Lassila's life became a horrific tragedy when a beloved threw sulfuric acid on him": https://www.is.fi/ kotimaa /art-2000005746278.html).

- In the teaser right below that title we are told that "Kun Algot Untolasta tuli kirjailija Maiju Lassila, hän oli kokenut miehenä ison menetyksen. Sen jälkeen hän erakoitui lukuisten salanimien taakse" ("When Algot Untola became writer Maiju Lassila, he had suffered a great loss as a man. After that he withdrew into isolation behind numerous pseudonyms").

- On the exterior wall at Runeberginkatu 6, Helsinki, there is a plaque proclaiming that Irmari Rantmala and Maiju Lassila lived in this building during their last years. The person who lived there, of course, was Algot Untola.

- The "Burial of Maiju Lassila" in the photograph on the back cover of this book was actually the burial of Algot Untola.

And so on. In Tohmajärvi, the small town in northern Karelia (close to what is now the Russian border) where the author was born, there is a Maiju Lassila Comprehensive School, a Maiju Lassila Street, and a monument to Maiju Lassila as the town's most famous resident—the heteronym! In late November, 2008, Tohmajärvi celebrated the 140th anniversary of the author's birth and 90th anniversary of his death with a "Maiju Lassila weekend." The 2019 campaign launched by the mayor's Russian husband to rename all Maiju Lassila memorabilia in town with the odd monicker "King of Zembla" was shouted down indignantly in the municipal council; as a sop to her humiliated spouse, the mayor pushed through a bill naming the Asematie ("Station St.") underpass under Highway 9 the "King of Zembla Tunnel."[3]

Interestingly, as Kaisa Kurikka points out in her 2013 doctoral dissertation "Algot Untola and the Writing Machine," the choice between calling Untola either "Irmari Rantamala" or "Maiju Lassila" falls along ideological lines: the right tends to call Untola Maiju Lassila, the left Irmari Rantamala.

Following that pattern, a novel (or other study) titled *The Last Days of Maiju Lassila* could very well deal explicitly and exclusively (but conservatively) with the author *and not* the heteronym.

As the tabloid teaser cited above suggests—"After that he withdrew into isolation behind numerous pseudonyms"—Untola's proliferation of heteronyms and pseudonyms has also been psychologized. Eino Railo (1884-1948), himself a Finnish novelist who published eleven books under pseudonyms, but who was also Untola's publisher, and who for some reason was an observer on the transport ship when Untola was executed—and makes a cameo appearance in this novel—wrote in

---

[3] I suggest we delete this sentence entirely. I have viewed that "underpass" on Google Street View, and it's actually an at-grade junction—there is no underpass. I suspect the line is a lame Nabokovian allusion that readers are unlikely to get. [Ed.]

1923 that Untola was a pathologically unhappy and uncommunicative personality who tragically never outgrew the shame and bitterness he suffered as a child, and so withdrew into complete isolation—hence not only the proliferation of pseudonyms but the refusal to meet his publishers face to face (he handled all interactions with publishers by mail, and signed his letters with the names of the relevant heteronyms) ... not to mention, of course, the sick attraction to leftist causes.

To be sure, whatever Railo's actual political orientation was, this condescending anti-leftist sentiment was still good protective coloring in 1923, five years after the Civil War. In 1948, four years after the conclusion of Finland's third war with its eastern neighbor and former colonizer, Mikko Saarenheimo diagnosed Untola with schizophrenia—a diagnosis that Kaisa Kurikka deftly turns into a positive by referring it to Deleuze and Guattari's schizanalysis, which was based on R. D. Laing's argument that schizophrenia is our only escape route from the schizoid condition that our society considers "normal." Presumably what Saarenheimo meant by "schizophrenia," though, was the popular conception of the disorder as generating "multiple personalities" (i.e., Dissociative Identity Disorder).

In addition to Maiju Lassila and J I Vatanen, Untola also wrote as Irmari Rantamala, A Rantala, Väinö Stenberg, Liisa Vatanen, Antti Iisalo, Liisan Antti ("Lisa's Andy"), Tanssi-Antti ("Dance Andy"), Sota-Antti ("War Andy"), Aino Kerpola, Jussi Porilainen—and many other names.[4] The female names in

---

[4] In addition, as in Pessoa's output, there are several characters in Untola's novels who are writers and so might be identified as proto-heteronyms: Baron Geldner (Irmari Rantamala's *Harhama* and *Martva*), Kynämö, Runosto, Mustemala, and Kirjamo (*Martva*), Artturi Turonen, Jussi Erhetyinen, and Lassi Maijula (Maiju Lassila's *Love*), and, in two unpublished novels by Liisa Vatanen—whom J I Vatanen in *The Last Days of Maiju Lassila* identifies as ta's pseudonym—Niilo Päivänheimo ("Fetching Water") and Uuno Korpi and Pekka Koponen ("Among the People"). [Tr.]

that list in addition to Maiju Lassila are Aino Kerpola and Liisa Vatanen (the latter claimed by J I Vatanen as ta's pseudonym for the unpublished novel "Veden haussa" ["Fetching Water"]). Jussi Vatanen is one of the two main characters in Maiju Lassila's 1910 novel *Tulitikkuja lainaamassa* ("Borrowing Matches," Untola's most popular novel), and that character could constitute a kind of heteronymic "biography" of J I Vatanen; but J I, like A in "A Rantala," is of course gender-neutral, and so is the invented name Irmari in "Irmari Rantamala," Untola's second-most-productive heteronym. *Ilmari* would be a male name, and a recent publisher of one of Maiju Lassila's previously unpublished novel manuscripts, Arto Pietilä, systematically referred in 2002 to "Ilmari Rantamala"; but Irma, Mari, and Irmeli would all be female names, and Irmari would appear to be Untola's nonce coinage combining all four. Juha Hurme, a brilliant playwright, novelist, and theater director who has staged several of Maiju Lassila's plays and written a play based on Untola's life, also cites the genital-destroying acid incident, but rather than pathologizing the use of heteronyms, notes that after the incident Untola never wrote under a male name again: rather, *sukupuoleltaan hän muuttui hybridiksi* "he became a gender hybrid." The acid incident unfolded as the conclusion to a bitter quarrel the day after Christmas, 1907, and Untola's first novel, *Harhama*, appeared a year and a half later, in 1909, under the Irmari Rantamala name—which of course is a gender-hybrid. Four more Rantamala novels appeared during Untola's lifetime. 1910 saw the publication of the first Maiju Lassila novel, *Tulitikkuja lainaamassa* ("Borrowing Matches"), and 14 more Maiju Lassila novels (and five Maiju Lassila plays) followed during the eight years Untola had left to live. Only a single novel, *Avuttomia* ("The Helpless Ones") was published under the gender-neutral J I Vatanen name, in 1913.

One other interesting link-up: Harhama, the name of the

protagonist in Irmari Rantamala's first two novels, *Harhama* and *Martva*, is a Finnish word for the genetic hybrid known as a chimera—an organism with cells from two or more geno-types, or, specifically in animals, derived from two or more zygotes. If the zygotes that mix are male and female, the result may be intersexuality—the presence of both male and female sex organs.[5] (One fairly common explanation of Untola's abandonment of his wife Therese Marie Johanna Küstring on their wedding day was that he discovered his bride was inter-sex. Nonnormative/post-binary sexuality is also an insistent thread running right through the *Last Days of Maiju Lassila* novel.)

In her doctoral dissertation on Untola's pennames, Kaisa Kurikka argues that Maiju Lassila was his only heteronym.

---

[5] But it may also result in oddities like male calico cats, feline chimeras born of one male zygote and one female calico zygote. The hybridity, in other words, may be in color rather than in genital shapes.

There are also chimera butterflies, famously studied by Vladimir Nabokov at Harvard, with one wing showing a typical female patterning and the other a typical male patterning. There is a little noticed line in the "Will o' the Wisp" chapter of Untola/Rantamala's *Harhama III* where "The children of nature danced innocently like *butterflies* on nature's pure bosom. *Harhama* ['Chimera'] stood at the window with Mrs. Esempion looking at the young folks' exuberant joy." Amusing, no?

In Finnish a *harha* is a delusion, a mirage, a hallucination; the *-ma* "ownership" ending tends to turn a verb into an adjective, as in *Rantamalan kirjoittama romaani* "the Rantamala-written novel," or "the novel written by Rantamala," from *kirjoittaa* "to write" and *romaani* "novel." Because *harhaa* isn't a verb, *harhama* doesn't work the same way, but it does suggest something like "deluded, hallucinated," as in "that's the religion I deluded," or "that's the religion born out of my delusion."

That's appropriate for the Faustian premise of the two Rantamala novels, certainly. But it's also appropriate for a pseudotranslation, whose "original" is not just a delusion but a nonexistent text "deluded" (imagined and projected *as* a delusion) by the pseudotranslator. [Tr.]

Harhama III? I thought only two volumes were ever published—that the third was lost? [Ed.]

Certainly, as we've seen, it was his most popular. But Kurikka claims that status for Maiju Lassila on the basis of the 1912 Maiju Lassila novel *Rakkautta* ("Love"), in which Maiju Lassila "herself" narrates an earlier love story from her young womanhood; and as we've seen, the portrayal of the middle-aged widower Jussi Vatanen in *Tulitikkuja/*"Matches" arguably serves the same purpose for J I Vatanen; and Maiju's twin brother the writer M Lassila and Irmari Rantamala feature prominently in the unfinished, unpublished, and unattributed novel manuscript "Ville Sorsan romaani" ("Ville Sorsa's Novel"). Maiju Lassila appears in a single paragraph there, as M Lassila's writer twin sister—but that too contributes to her heteronymic biography. Arguably, therefore, Untola had *four* heteronyms—one of whom, M Lassila, never appeared as the named author of one of his novels.

In translating this novel I have endeavored—as of course translators almost inevitably do—to stick as closely as I can to the Finnish original. In one area, however, that has proved difficult, namely, the singular third-person personal pronoun. In Finnish there is only one: *hän* is a gender-neutral s/he, indicating a human being of any gender, or many, or none. Since three of the main characters in *The Last Days of Maiju Lassila*, including the twins Maiju and M Lassila and the narrator and pseudonymous author J I Vatanen—and, at the end, Irmari Rantamala as well—self-identify as gender-neutral or post-binary in some unspecified way, presumably transgender or intersex, it is obviously essential for the English translator to honor the gender-neutrality of the third-person pronoun *hän*—but how?

In translating passages from Finnish transgender novels for my 2019 book *Transgender, Translation, Translingual*

Address I opted for the invented gender-neutral pronouns *ze* and *zir*—and in fact, somewhat controversially, generalized those gender-neutral pronouns to every human being mentioned in the book, including people who would have insisted that they use he/him or she/her pronouns.

Because of the queering effect of what Douglas Hofstadter calls "strange loops," too, in my 2022 book *The Strange Loops of Translation* I first used *ze/zir* pronouns for everybody, and then, when reviewers for the press protested this practice rather intensely, after some thought I decided to use *they/them* pronouns. But then the question remained: should I use them for everybody, or should I try to honor each individual's preference? I decided in the end to reframe *all* personal identity along strange-loops lines: Hofstadter's great cogsci innovation is that convergences of the layered analogies by which "I" both do something and observe "my" "self" doing that thing are *constitutive* of the "I"—the self, or personal identity—and while he doesn't explicitly take this next step and insist on the inevitable *multiplicity* of the "I," his good friend Daniel Dennett does, in a book Hofstadter cites twice in *I Am a Strange Loop*. Dennett's term is the "pandemonial" self: thousands of word-demons and tone-demons and so on launch themselves ballistically into competition each time for the right to voice the "I" that says "I." So as I set things up there, Douglas Hofstadter doesn't write his books and theorize strange loops: the multiple and often multiply/mutually (self-)contradictory demons of the Douglas Hofstadter Pandemonium do. And in referring to the DHP I use *they/them* pronouns. I also use *they/them* pronouns for the Daniel Dennett Pandemonium (DDP), and even, sometimes, for the Douglas Robinson Pandemonium (DRP)—whenever I speak of what the DRP demons were trying to do in some earlier book. Whenever I speak for the DRP in the present tense, I use we/us pronouns. The same applies for every other human pandemonial self mentioned in the book.

Rather than exploring that post-binary plural pronoun for singular persons here, however, I settled on a different tactic—one you will not have seen anywhere else, in fact. It was suggested to me by my colleague at the Chinese University of Hong Kong, Shenzhen, the novelist Melvin Sterne, after he read the novel in manuscript and expressed some qualms about my *they/them* pronouns for the four nonbinary heteronyms. Melvin said: "Don't the Chinese use *ta* for he, she, and it?" I liked the sound of that—even though Chinese intellectuals had successfully lobbied for different characters to represent *ta*/he, *ta*/she, and *ta*/it back in the early decades of the twentieth century, the pronoun had been undifferentiated for gender or animateness for several millennia before that, and still today all three are pronounced exactly the same. The Chinese form the possessive with the particle *de* (*ta de*/his, *ta de*/her(s), *ta de*/its), but that can all be *ta's* in English. The pronoun remains unchanged as a direct or indirect object in Chinese, and I decided to do the same in English.

One other thing about the translation: there are those who frown on the use of annotations in translations. Everything the target reader needs to know, they say, should go into a slightly expanded and more explanatory version of the text. However, since there is considerable historical and other cultural knowledge here to which English-speaking readers with no Finnish would have no access—and indeed Russian-era cultural details from a century and more ago that most contemporary Finns would not know—I have reluctantly decided to provide explanations in endnotes. I hope they prove more useful than not.

If the copious Algot Untola (aka Maiju Lassila!) scholarship sheds a good deal of light on the novel that you hold in your hands, this "Vatanen" novel also sheds an interesting light on the heteronymic complexities of Untola's output to which it alludes, and with which it plays. But, having said that, I'm afraid I must conclude this Translator's Preface by stepping ever so gently on an amusing if ill-conceived line of speculation launched by a zealous Finnish critic from the University of Nuorgam in northern Lapland, my nemesis, one Prof. Julius Nyrkki.[6] His brief is that

(a) the supposed source text for this translation doesn't actually exist, making this not a translation but a pseudotranslation;

(b) both J I Vatanen and Maiju Lassila were heteronyms used by Algot Untola (1868-1918), which means that Vatanen could not possibly have written a memoir of "the last days of Maiju Lassila," after Untola's death;

(c) the basic premise of the work as it appears here is uncannily reminiscent of the great 1984 novel by the Portuguese novelist and 1998 Nobel Laureate José Saramago, *O Ano da Morte de Ricardo Reis*, translated into English in 1991 by Giovanni Pontiero as *The Year of the Death of Ricardo Reis*; and

(d) the fact that several of my phrasings in English resonate "suspiciously" with similar phrasings in Pontiero's translation of Saramago suggests that this is actually not a translation of a "nonexistent" Finnish original but an adaptation of Pontiero's English translation of Saramago's novel.

---

[6] Can we please get a fact check on this guy's university? I find Dr. Nyrkki himself in Google Scholar, with a few dozen citations, but the only significant institution Wikipedia names in Nourgam (sp?) would appear from the photos to be an amusement park called Kalle Kakkonen. And typesetter, don't set these editorial notes. [Ed.]

"Kalle Kakkonen" in English is "Charles II." Just saying. [Tr.]

Whoa, Nellie!

Unfortunately for (a), the unpublished novel manuscript "Maiju Lassilan viimeiset päivät" (1922), literally "Maiju Lassila's last days," does unquestionably exist—as I say, in the Algot Untola/Maiju Lassila archive at the National Library of Finland, with the penciled-in "1922" as the presumed date of authorship. To be sure, the Finnish Wikipedia page for Algot Untola has no mention of the novel; but then it mentions none of the dozens of other unpublished manuscripts that are stored under the Algot Untola/Maiju Lassila name in the National Library, either. And it is likely that Prof. Nyrkki, because he works at Finland's northernmost university, was unable to make the 1300 km (780 mi) trek down to the National Library in Helsinki to see the manuscript for himself. Pity.

As for (b): *no duh*, as the kids say. I see no effort here to hide the obvious fact that the Untola heteronym J I Vatanen as invoked in 1922 is a *pseudonym*, not for the four-years-dead Untola but for some other Finnish novelist. Like many a novel before it—indeed like "the novel" as a genre in modern literary history—*Maiju Lassilan viimeiset päivät*, which I've translated fairly unimaginatively as *The Last Days of Maiju Lassila*, is a novel *pretending* to be a memoir. The fact that neither Vatanen nor Lassila was a "real person" is about as devastating for its status as a novel as the fact that the narrator and pseudonymous author Lemuel Gulliver was not a real person was for Swift. Prof. Nyrkki here joins the illustrious company of the bishop who declared angrily in 1726, upon reading "Lemuel Gulliver's" "memoir," *Gulliver's Travels*, "I personally believe every word in this book to be a damned lie."

And there is a very simple explanation for (c) and (d): I was reading Saramago's novel in Pontiero's English translation first, and its premise reminded me of the stories a Finnish friend had told me of the legendary novel about (and "by") Untola's heteronyms—which I had never read. It took me a few months to track it down, but I finally located the world's only copy in the National Library in Helsinki; on my next visit to Finland, then, I went to the National Library and read the first few chapters of the novel, and had photocopies made of both it and the other novel manuscripts in the collection in which Untola's heteronyms figure prominently, the anonymous "Ville Sorsan romaani" ("Ville Sorsa's novel") and "Veden haussa" ("Fetching Water," by Liisa Vatanen). In fact, of course, the Vatanen/Untola/Lassila novel tells a very different story than does the Saramago/Pessoa/Reis novel;[7] all the two have in common, really, is the remarkable premise that originally caught my eye, that a literary heteronym survives ta's author's death but has

---

[7] In Saramago's novel Ricardo Reis hears of Fernando Pessoa's recent death from Álvaro de Campos and decides to return to Lisbon after an eighteen-year absence in Brazil. For the next eight or so months he meets people, including Pessoa's ghost (who explains that the dead are allowed nine months to wander around their old environs before heading off to the afterlife—the one significant plot detail that "Vatanen's" novel shares with Saramago's), and then dies, which apparently means going off with Pessoa at the end of his post-mortem nine months. He also develops an impossible crush on a sixteen-year-old girl with a withered left hand, gets involved sexually with a hotel chambermaid, moves into an apartment, works for a few months as a doctor, all the while going for long walks around Lisbon; none of this happens in "Vatanen's" book.

There are also significant differences between the two dead authors' return from the dead. The dead Fernando Pessoa can't read, casts a shadow but can't see himself in a mirror, and can only be seen by the living if he wills it; the dead Algot Untola inhabits an ectoplasmic body that can be seen by everybody and reads as well as any living human. The dead Fernando Pessoa and Ricardo Reis talk about the ultimate questions, what it means to be dead, what it means to be alive; the dead Algot Untola is mostly obsessed with revenge. But then that obsession arises out of the horrendous violence by which Untola was "legally" murdered, and that violence is visited in turn on his ectoplasmic body and, through phantom pain, on the bodies of two of his heteronyms, Maiju Lassila and Irmari Rantamala. Saramago's novel is a philosophical reflection on life and death, culture and eternity; "Vatanen's" novel is a socio-psychological reflection on intergenerational trauma. [Tr.]

conversations with the author's ghost.

And in any case, it seems to me that the true model for this novel's plot—the second half, anyway, "After"—is not Saramago's *Reis*, which postdates it by a good half century, but one of the novels that Algot Untola published under the Maiju Lassila name: *Kuolleista herännyt* (Otava, 1916).

In English that would be "The Revenant."

Les beaux livres sont écrits dans une sorte de langue étrangère. Sous chaque mot chacun de nous met son sens ou du moins son image qui est souvent un contresens. Mais dans les beaux livres, tous les contresens qu'on fait sont beaux.
—Marcel Proust, "Conclusion," *Contre Sainte-Beuve* (written in 1908[8])

Beautiful books are written in a sort of foreign language. On each word each of us imposes our own meaning, or at least our own image, which is often a mistranslation. But in beautiful books, all of the mistranslations made there are beautiful.
—(translated from the French by DR)

Ja sama pätee tuplaten banaaleihin kirjoihin.
—J I Vatanen

And the same goes double for banal books.
—(translated from the Finnish by DR)

---

[8] While Proust did indeed begin in 1908 to write the essays that were eventually collected as *Contre Sainte-Beuve*, it is unlikely that the conclusion quoted here was written then, and the entire collection was not published in French until 1954, 32 years after Proust's death. Since the manuscript of this Finnish novel is marked in pencil on the cover sheet and once inside the novel as well as having been written (or at least finished) in 1922, the year Proust died, it is at least within the realm of possibility (though perhaps not of plausibility) that the author could have read the unpublished French text and quoted from it here; but J I Vatanen never gives us any indication that ta can read French, and the Finnish translation was not published until 2003. (It appeared in Sylvia Townsend Warner's English translation, under the title *By Way of Sainte Beuve*, just four years after the initial posthumous French publication, in 1958.)

Those essays, of course, were what inspired Proust to start writing *À la recherche du temps perdu*, the next year, in 1909—it was supposed to disprove Sainte-Beuve's theory that biography is the best way to understand an artist's work. Proust's alternative, as everyone knows, was the memoir-novel. But what if the best way is actually a *pseudotranslation* of a memoir-novel? [Tr.]

0

PROLOGUE

Maiju Lassila died in 1919. I've called this the story of ta's last days, but in fact it's a memoir of the two and a half decades I knew ta.[9] The war was over in mid-May, 1918, and then the White Terror began. They took Algot almost a week later, shot him up, pushed him into the Gulf of Finland to see how well a dead man could swim. Algot Untola, Maiju and M's friend from Tohmajärvi, who agitated for the Reds in the war and was executed without a trial by the rampaging Whites when they won. I'll tell that story too, along the way. It's the pivot of this book. Algot came back from the dead, for a while. Maiju and I met him after he returned from the dead, and I can confirm that he was substantially embodied—as he insisted, *not* a ghost—and that there were no bullet holes in his palms or anywhere else visible. He himself bragged that his genitals were restored, and offered to show us; but we declined. So I can't vouch for that. Frankly, I didn't like to be around a dead man.

---

[9] "Vatanen" here has "Tämä on tarina *hänen* viimeisistä päivistään" ("This is a/the story of his/her last days"), and "muistelmat niistä kahdesta ja puolesta vuosikymmenestä, joina *hänet* tunsin" ("a memoir of the two and a half decades I knew him/her"). Finnish *hän*—here first in the possessive, *hänen*, then in the accusative, *hänet*—is the third-person personal pronoun that covers both "he" and "she" in Finnish. Because as Vatanen says they both were of indeterminate gender, and were at various times mistaken for either men or women, it seemed important not to impose either he/him or she/her pronouns on either; instead, I've used *ta* pronouns for both, and each. [Tr.]

Sure, I was superstitious. So what? Not a crime.

It was around the time Algot said he had to go, and wouldn't be back, that Maiju died of an opium overdose. Some of the others went around then as well. As far as I know I'm the only one left. But more about that anon.

So yes, Maiju and I lived together for a quarter century. And we were close.

In fact there were those, back in the day, before we had to go into hiding, and go out only in even more radical disguise—whisperers, scandal-mongers, clueless colleagues of ours in the theater, which was a surprisingly conservative institution around the turn of the century—who called us Sapphic lovers. And, believe it or not, there were others—insecure young men in the street, mostly, seeing us walking hand in hand—who called us Sodomites. That's some kind of testimony to the confusion we sowed. By the way we dressed, I suppose, but not just that. The way we walked. The way we moved our hands. The way we pursed our lips and rolled our eyes. We were actors, of course. Maiju and I knew how to do male and female, masculine and feminine, butch and femme—and we knew how to do indeterminate, the beyonds, the in-betweens.

But we were never lovers. Not that way. We loved each other, yes. But our love was always more textual than sexual. We never had the slightest hankering to take our clothes off together. With anybody, in fact. That just never seemed worth the effort, to either of us.

Call us strange.

You best know Maiju as the author of *Borrowing Matches*, ta's first novel, published in 1910. That put ta on the cultural map.

I'm sure you remember how popular it was; you probably have a copy on your bookshelf at home. You may also remember the government wanting to give ta a major literary award for it, and Maiju saying thanks but no thanks, ta was just a popular entertainer, not some high-falutin' novelist. What you may not know is that between *Borrowing Matches* in 1910 and ta's death in 1919 Maiju published a total of *twenty* books, including fifteen works of fiction and five plays, and left umpteen book manuscripts unpublished at ta's death, more than 4000 pages' worth, including a thing called "Ville Sorsa's Novel" featuring ta's identical twin, M, also a writer, or a would-be writer, and Irmari Rantamala. You probably remember the real-life Rantamala from the massive philosophical novels ta published in 1909, *Harhama* and *Martva*, ta's decadent *Faust* I and II.

Me? I've published one novel, *one*, a short 1913 novel called *Avuttomia*, meaning "The Helpless Ones." I also wrote a couple of other novels as Liisa Vatanen, back before the war, but never got them published. Well, one of them I never even finished. The other one, "Veden haussa" ("Fetching Water"), was rejected by the publisher as too vulgar. He didn't like the farting and the leg-scratching and generally the "naturalism" of people doing what people do—exactly what that protofascist bully August Ahlqvist said about Kivi's *Brothers Seven*, and why that book, the greatest novel ever written in Finnish, shouldn't be published.[10] My Ahlqvist was a guy named Kyösti

---

[10] Aleksis Kivi (1834-1872), born Alexis Stenvall, was effectively the creator of modern Finnish literature, with his 1864 play *Nummisuutarit* (which I translated in 1993 as *Heath Cobblers*) and his 1870 novel *Seitsemän veljestä* (which I translated in 2020 as *The Brothers Seven*). August Ahlqvist attacked the novel viciously in print three times, twice in Swedish and once in Finnish; it is generally agreed that his attacks drove Kivi to an early death at 38. Ahlqvist was not only the only professor of Finnish literature but the acknowledged bastard son of Finland's most powerful man, the equivalent of a prime minister, who had been tasked by the tsar with keeping an eye on seditious behavior in the Finnish Grand Duchy.

Wilkuna. We'll see him again in the story.

Next to Maiju Lassila, frankly, I was always the helpless one. Ta's books too were criticized as too "naturalistic"—but ta managed to get most of them into print, where ta was hailed critically as a great folk humorist.

One more observation and we'll get started. You may remember Antti Ihalainen's friend in *Borrowing Matches*, the farmer who asks Antti to come help him woo a new wife and so distracts him from the match-borrowing errand for the entire novel—a helpless or hapless fellow named Jussi Vatanen. That was Maiju's little joke. Name the comic loser in ta's first novel after me (sort of), make him a young man with a potato nose who can't do anything right.[11] Jussi—Johnny—is not my first name. And I'm not a man.

But so, anyway, turnabout is fair play. In "Fetching Water," writing as Liisa Vatanen, I fictionalized Maiju Lassila's transformation into a prolific novelist—under the name of Maiju Laurila. And just as Maiju had caricatured me as a male

---

If you enjoy my translation of this memoir-novel, you may also enjoy my renditions of Kivi's play and novel. The novel and my heteronymous transcreation of Volter Kilpi's unfinished posthumous novel *Gulliver's Voyage to Phantomimia* are both available from zetabooks.com. [Tr.]

Note to legal: are we allowed to promote the releases of other publishers? Please look into it. I think we probably want to kill that last paragraph. [Ed.]

[11] Actually, Jussi Vatanen is described in that novel not as a young man but as *kuudennella kymmenellä* "in his sixth decade," which is to say in his fifties. He is perceived by the others in the book as a fairly well-established dairy farmer—he has fifteen milking cows. What does it signify that the pseudonymous author has missed the estimation of Jussi's age as fifty-something on the second page of the novel? (Surprisingly, the discussion of Jussi's potato-shaped nose comes *after* the discussion of his age.) [Tr.]

rube in *Borrowing Matches*, I caricatured Maiju in "Fetching Water" as a snobbish heiress who despises crofters and other peasants as barnyard animals, and shudders at the thought of portraying them in the novel she's writing:

> I groan at the thought of depicting these people now, sprinkling them into the flowerbed of nature's great beauty. I pity them and would prefer not to reveal their ugliness, show them that they are natural creatures. I was planning to paint them with <u>false</u> colors, beautiful colors, decorate them—but I can't. I can't be dishonest, for dishonesty has no part in beauty. All nature is honestly and truly itself, and that is what makes it beautiful. Beauty is noble and dishonesty is ignoble, and therefore cannot be art.

In the opening pages of that unpublished novel, I have Maiju reflect on the crofter Olli Turunen and his family, despising them as deplorable beasts of burden that are incapable even of rising to the level of Noble Savages; she longs to find a single bright pearl in the peasantry, a noble individual that she might make the hero of her story.

I never discussed this with my Maiju; ta read it and laughed at my caricature, but we didn't pull the novel apart to decipher my class-based feelings and attitudes—any more than we did ta's in *Borrowing Matches*.

As I was writing that Liisa Vatanen novel, though, I did intermittently harbor the gnawing suspicion that Maiju was precisely that upper-class snob, who did tolerate and even love me because in ta's eyes I was the noble exception, the actor, the writer—the artist, who miraculously rose out of vile peasant bestiality into the cultured class.

Abject confession: I was grateful. I thought I was the

luckiest crofter's kid alive.

Even more abject confession: I wasn't entirely sure that I *was* alive.

BEFORE

(1875 – early May, 1918)

1

Well, all right, I confess I exaggerated a bit when I identified with the "helpless ones" in the title of my sole published novel—but only a bit. That novel is about a crofter family named the Varises, the Crows, who are evicted off their croft—

> And it had indeed been a heavy-hearted night, this last night. Only yesterday had they finally, irrevocably heard that they were to be evicted from the croft. Ville Hukka,[12] on whose land the shack stood, was being kicked off the stead as well. Indebted, impoverished, he had had to sell more than half of his farm. This shack of theirs was on the section that was to be sold, and the buyer was planning to build his new house on the site where their shack now stood. All the previous day had this thought weighed upon them, and it had kept them from sleep till past midnight. Only now, on the very ear of morning, had exhaustion and sleep triumphed for a moment.

---

[12] The primary meaning of Hukka is "loss" or "waste," as in *valua hukkaan* "go to waste" or *olla hukassa* "be lost." It's not a common surname; Vatanen seems to have invented it as an allegorical indicator of the character's situation. But its secondary meaning is a colloquial endearment for a wolf, as in a children's fable: a *susihukka* might here be the predator who is feared by all farmers but has fallen on hard times and so is deserving of our pity. [Tr.]

—and while I did grow up a crofter's kid, up in the flatlands of Ostrobothnia, we were not evicted, and I was lucky: the landowner we rented from took a liking to me and sent me to school, first for two years in our village, then for three years in Nikolainkaupunki or Nikolaistad (before 1855 and since 1918 called Vaasa), then for four final years in Helsinki. I got an education. I got out.

"I" got out. My good fortune never quite felt real to me. It was as if it was happening to someone else, and I was just there as a pair of eyes on the wall. Helpless—and not quite helpless. The gap between the two beyond my control.

On Nikolaistad and Vaasa: early in the Civil War the Whites took Nikolaistad and restored it to its Finnish name Vaasa,[13] set up their headquarters there. They called it the capital of independent Finland. As the war was breaking out the Senate fled Red-controlled Helsinki to Vaasa and convened there during the war, till the Germans arrived in mid-April, retook Helsinki in just two days, and the Senate moved back down.

On crofters: we, they—crofters—became a political hot potato around the turn of the century, largely because the landowners started escalating their demands, raising rents, requiring punitive overtime farming, and more and more refusing to renew tenancies. Life became very hard for crofters, almost unbearable. There were crofter strikes and infamous evictions, and crofters began to organize. In 1906 the first general meeting of crofters was held, and the demands that came out of that began to put pressure on the Diet to legislate protection for crofters. In 1909 a law was passed improving conditions, including mandatory written leases

---

[13] Well, technically Swedish: the Finnish town was named after the Vasa royal family, which had ruled Sweden (and Poland) in the sixteenth and seventeenth centuries. Hence presumably the Russian desire to rename it after Tsar Nikolai I (1796-1855) upon his death. [Tr.]

with a minimum lease period of fifty years—but not the right to buy out a croft, which the crofters had demanded. Some say it was the growing political tension between crofters and landowners, and not the oppressive Russification measures that began in 1899, that was the main reason for the Civil War. In fact at the time some called that war the Crofter Rebellion. Who knows? Maybe. My mother told me the crofters from our village who fought on the Red side in the war were forced to join up. In any case, a law finally giving crofters the right to buy out their crofts was passed two months after the end of the war, in the summer of 1918.

Because of my family background, I cared about those political tensions as much as I cared about anything (outside of Maiju). I poured those feelings into my novel about "The Helpless Ones."

One reviewer called it the best writing about the Finnish underclasses ever. So I'm not entirely helpless.

If that was really me.

2

My education took place in the 1880s. I was born in 1875, began my school at age six in 1881, and was graduated from the lyceum in Helsinki in 1890, at the age of 14. I was admitted into the very first cohort of Finland's first Finnish-language lyceum in 1886. *Suomalainen Yhteiskoulu,* SYK: the Finnish Coeducational School. Coeducation was a radical new idea back then. It caught on later, of course, partly inspired by SYK. I lived in a drafty apartment with a distant cousin of my mother in the Helsinki district of Rödbergen, Red Mountain, which we called Rööperi. It was a working-class neighborhood of ramshackle wooden buildings; the cold wet winter winds swept through them as if it were trying to blow them down. My mother's cousin resented having to board me for free, and hardly fed me; I lived on a crust of bread and a shriveled potato a day, plus whatever I could scrounge from the cooks I befriended at local eateries. A lot of shady-looking people were always coming around to his place, too, which made me think maybe he resented having to take me in because he was involved in some things that he didn't want outsiders witnessing.

His place was fairly close to the school, though, or to the various locations in Kamppi the school occupied temporarily while I was there—a fifteen- or twenty-minute walk each way. So it wasn't all bad.

One of my fellow students at SYK was Mia Backman, who

later became a great mover and shaker on the Finnish theater scene, first acting in Swedish-language theaters, then taking over as director of the People's Stage, formerly the Workers' Theater. Her theatrical career and mine never quite intersected, but in school she took a liking to me—I was just enough of a cuckoobird to appeal to her love of the warped and the weird—and she was the one who first got me interested in theater. She made me read great plays in German and Russian and English, and dragged me to performances at the Finnish Theater, which had only been in operation for a little over a decade then, over on Arkadiankatu, in the Arkadia Theater building, not far from our school. She taught me to sneak into performances without paying: she was as poor as I was. I especially remember a young Ida Aalberg as Margareta in Goethe's *Faust*, as Camille in Musset's *No Trifling with Love*, and as Saint Joan in Schiller's *Maid of Orleans*. The Goethe and the Musset were at the end of our first year, the Schiller at the beginning of our second—and then Mia quit school and started acting.

I stayed in school, but had also caught the bug. When Aurora Aspegren and her husband August Aspegren, who had been major players at the Finnish Theater, pulled out in 1887 and founded the Aspegrens' Finnish People's Theater, I started spending my free time there. I was twelve. Mia had left school by then. I did whatever odd jobs the Aspegrens would let me do. I swept, picked up trash, helped carry props. Sometimes they would let me man the box office. A farmer's kid, I knew how to drive a nail and slap on paint, so gradually they started letting me build scenery. They didn't pay me, but sometimes they would hand me a bag of food.

And I watched rehearsals. And they let me into performances for free. I couldn't imagine a better situation. I saw Wecksell's *Daniel Hjort*, with Mrs. Aspegren as Katri. In Kivi's *Betrothal* she played the female lead, the Gentlemen's Eeva, and her husband was Aapeli, the hapless tailor that Eeva disastrously recruits as her fiancé to make the gentlemen she works for jealous.[14] I watched them first rehearse, then perform Molière's *Tartuffe*, and was entranced. This was theater!

By the time I finished school in 1890, I had made myself indispensable to the Aspegrens, and they agreed to start paying me a few Finnish marks a week. A pittance, but it was enough to buy a week's larder in the Hakaniemi Market—a round rye loaf, four smoked herring, a chunk of butter in paper, and a brown bottle of milk—and I began to put on some weight. Not that I became fat: just less painfully skinny. One of the other stagehands had showed me some exercises, too, push-ups, sit-ups, star-jumps, and the like, and I did them faithfully every day. I was already in training to be an actor. I kept up the reading regimen Mia Backman had set me, too: the Helsinki People's Library on Rikhardinkatu made a triangle with home and work, and I stopped there almost every morning to check out plays. I devoured them, in all the languages they had taught us at SYK.

Soon I was begging the Aspegrens to put me on stage in crowd scenes, and they did. And when I didn't embarrass myself or others, they began to give me small speaking roles. By the time I was eighteen I was acting full-time, every night, twice on Sundays. I was in heaven. Life couldn't possibly get any better than this!

---

[14] For my English translation of this classic 1866 one-act play by Aleksis Kivi, see "The Troth-Plight," in *Aleksis Kivi and/as World Literature* (Brill, 2017). [Tr.] Legal: *please.* [Ed.]

3

The more money I made, too, the better I could afford to spend whatever nights off I had attending performances back at the Finnish Theater—and one night there, in my twentieth year, I met my future. It was a performance of Shakespeare's *Comedy of Errors*, which I had read in English. But someone, probably Kaarlo Bergbom, the director, or maybe his sister Emilie, had adapted the play to make the slave twins, both named Dromio in the original, not boys but girls.[15] The two sets of identical twins are Antipholus and Antipholus, the masters, and Dromia and Dromia, the (female) slaves. Why would they do that— whoever the dramaturg was? Because they had a pair of identical twins on staff in the theater, and for those twins gender was a kind of bravura number. The one playing the Dromia twins was done up as a woman, of course, or as two women, but it was still clear that there were in effect *four* twins on stage. (Maybe they switched genders during intermission? Impossible to tell!)

I left the theater that night not knowing the twins' names, but they haunted my imagination for weeks—months. I went back to see a production of Chekhov's *Three Sisters* three or

---

[15] This is almost certainly fiction. The first Finnish translation of the *Comedy of Errors* anyone knows of in the real world is Paavo Cajander's *Hairauksia*, which was published in 1910, fifteen or so years after this supposed production by the Finnish Theater. [Tr.]

four months later,[16] and found that Maria and Irina had again been made twins, and the playscript retranslated or rewritten accordingly. Again those two twins absolutely possessed me.

Why? I'm not exactly sure. They weren't exactly vivacious, in the style of the day. They didn't play to the audience. They seemed to be holding back, staying inside their own bodies, not expanding their bodies to encompass the house—and yet they also seemed to be lit by some inner fire, an energizing spark that we all could feel.

Or, well, I did. Watching them was the touch of God's finger on me. I felt more alive than I had ever felt before.

This time, I couldn't help myself. After the show I went backstage to find them. They were taller than I had imagined—taller than me. Identical slim builds, identical short shag hair styles—dark hair, more Karelian than Finnish. They had identically colored eyes, a grayish green that shone with the same odd light.

I introduced myself. They introduced themselves: Maiju and M Lassila.

"M?" I said—instantly appalled as I heard the question come too quickly and too forwardly out of my mouth.

"J I?" one came back with a grin.

"Fair enough," I grinned sheepishly in return.

"I'm Maiju," the other one said. "Look at me closely."

I did.

"Now look at me," the other one said. "I'm M. Study me. Study the small differences."

I did that as well. And sure enough, I found some. I memorized them.

"Got it," I said.

---

[16] More fiction, presumably to support the starring roles of the identical twins Maiju and M Lassila. In J I Vatanen's retelling, this performance of Chekhov's *Three Sisters* would have taken place in 1895; but *Three Sisters* didn't premier until 1901, in the Moscow Art Theater. [Tr.]

"Good for you," Maiju said.

A beat. Then:

"You know," M said. "You haven't asked us the usual question."

"What question?"

"'Are you boys or girls?'"

I thought about that for a moment.

"I guess I assumed," I said finally, "that your answer would be the same as the one I always give."

"Which would be?"

"'Neither.'"

The two twins exchanged significant glances. And when I say *significant*, I mean earth-shaking. That was the moment when everything changed.

They turned back to me.

"Who are you, exactly?" M asked. "Where do you work?"

"The Finnish People's Theater."

"You're an actor too?"

"Yes."

"What are you doing after?" Maiju asked.

"Whatever you're doing."

Both nodded. And it was settled. We were friends.

We went back to their place in Katajanokka and talked all night. It was the greatest night of my young life.

4

Maiju and M came from a so-called "good" family. Their ancestors had been high officials since Finland had belonged to Sweden, almost a century before. They were from Tohmajärvi in northern Karelia, where their father had been the sheriff—a post that, as you know, always went to the scion of a local wealthy family.[17] Less than a year before I met the sheriff's twins, however, he had been appointed to the Aulic Council[18]

---

[17] In some cases the position as sheriff (in Finnish *vallesmanni* or *nimismies*) was inherited, passed from father to son for many generations; but technically the sheriff was appointed by the provincial governor. Sheriffs were wealthy commoners, not aristocrats—but their elevated status in society made them seem to other commoners like aristocrats. They were charged with keeping the peace, but also with organizing transport and lodging for high officials (and prisoners), tax-collection, and the so-called *käräjät*, which usually constituted a kind of law court but could be a gathering of all the wealthier, more educated, and more respected members of a community to decide anything. They were also entitled to tax-free income, making the job even more attractive. [Tr.]

[18] The Aulic Council (*Consilium Aulicum* in Latin, *Reichshofrat* in German) was originally one of two supreme courts in the Holy Roman Empire, but when that empire was conquered and annulled by Napoleon in 1808, the Aulic Council went as well. The Russian Empire, however, maintained their Aulic Council for another century, under the name Надворний совет/*Nadvorny sovyet*, until the massive political changes in 1917. Maiju and M's father's rank in Russian was Надворний советник/*Nadvorny sovyetnik*, in Finnish *hovineuvos*. [Tr.]

as a court councilor—in the Russian Table of Ranks an official of the seventh rank. In Russia officials of the *sixth* rank were automatically raised to the peerage, so all officials at the twins' father's rank were still commoners; but you may remember that in the Russian Grand Duchy of Finland, until independence in 1917, the old system of Swedish nobility still held sway, and no one could be raised to the peerage based on an official appointment. That high appointment had occasioned the family's move to Helsinki, where their father had been given an equivalent-rank job at the Imperial Baltic Fleet's Marine Barracks there in Katajanokka, as Captain Second Rank. Maiju and M smiled as they told me that if I were to meet him, I would have to address him as Your Honor.[19]

It was about that time, in the wee hours of the morning, as the summer sun was coming up, that I saw a large ship gliding past the open door out onto the twins' balcony, out in the North Harbor. I stood up, stretched, and walked to the door. I looked askance back at Maiju and M; when they nodded, I stepped out onto the balcony and watched the huge military vessel motor past, left to right.

Maiju stepped out onto the balcony alongside me, leaned against the stone balustrade.

"Battleship," ta said.

"What?"

"That's a Russian battleship. Half the Baltic Fleet is moored or anchored here on Katajanokka."

"Huh," I said. What did a crofter's kid know about Russian battleships, let alone the Baltic Fleet? One thing did occur to

---

[19] In Russian Ваше высокоблагородие. [Au.] Romanized, that Russian honorific would be *Vashe vysokoblagorodiye* (lit. "your high well-bornness"); the official Finnish equivalent that "Vatanen" used is *Teidän korkeasukuisuutenne* (lit. "your high kinship"). It sounds vastly more pompous in Finnish and Russian than the official English equivalent "Your Honor." [Tr.]

me to ask, though: "Where's it coming from?"

"What?"

"I mean, where could it possibly have been, over there to the left? Not much water that way. Did someone hitch a ride on it to the Uspensky Cathedral?"

"Oh, that," ta laughed. "No, it's usually anchored right out in front of us, bow pointing west, in toward Kruununhaka. They just make a little loop around in front of the Cathedral to turn it around before heading out to sea."

The apartment was on the fifth (top) floor of a brownstone facing north across Laivastokatu, Finnish for "Fleet Street," across to the islands and port structures in North Harbor. The view in that early morning light was magical. There's really no other word for it. I couldn't believe I was standing there, leaning against the stone balustrade on such a morning, next to such a person, looking out at such a view. I stood there silent for a long time, feeling the feelings I was feeling, letting myself experience the full shivery strangeness and wonderfulness of my life at that moment. That battleship out there was only the most extraordinarily surprising part of a most extraordinary circumstance.

"It's odd," I said finally, my eyes still out on the water. "I'd never given much thought to the Russian colonial power."

"What's there to think about?"

"I don't know, they rule the country, right? We're a Grand Duchy under them. They're the bosses. They make the big decisions about us. And yet—"

"And yet it doesn't occur to you to think about them much?"

"Exactly. What about you? Do you think about the Russians?"

"I've been thinking about them more and more since we moved here," Maiju said. "With Dad doing what he does, and all. But I know what you mean. When we lived up in Toh-majärvi I never thought about Finland being ruled by Russians."

"And having Russian warships sailing around Helsinki."

"Wait till you see the Baltic Fleet's Marine Barracks," ta said with a smile. "It's pretty impressive. Right over there," ta added, pointing to the right. "About three blocks down Laivastokatu."

"And your father works there. Your father is part of the Russian colonial power."

"Yes, he is." Ta looked over at me. "How does that make you feel about us? Do you hate us for it?"

"Not at all!" I cried, blushing a little at the passion behind my outburst, and at the thought that Maiju might think the worse of me for it. I felt way out of my league here. "I, uh—I feel like—" What did I feel like, exactly? Um—"like Russia is even more interesting because it's somehow linked to you."

"You do? Really?"

"I really do." This felt right, now. The more I thought about it, the truer it seemed. "I studied Russian at school. We read Pushkin's poems, Griboyedov's *Woe from Wit*, Chekhov's *Ivanov*,[20] stories by Lermontov and Turgenev and Dostoevsky.

---

[20] *Ivanov* was Chekhov's first play, written for and produced at the Korsh Theater in Moscow in the fall of 1887, the first semester of the narrator's and pseudonymous author's second year at SYK. The play was a failure, though, and it was only when a revised version was produced in St. Petersburg two years later and was a hit that Chekhov's career as a playwright was launched. This timeline leaves only a few months for Chekhov's playscript to migrate from St. Petersburg to Helsinki and find its way into the hands of the first cohort of final-year students of Russian literature at SYK—but then Finland was a Grand Duchy of Russia, and there were very close ties between St. Petersburg and Helsinki (the two capitals) in those days. It is not completely unreasonable to imagine that a Russian teacher at Finland's premier Finnish-language private school should have had access to the script of a recent hit on the Petersburg stage. [Tr.]

I loved all that. But I never thought of Russia *ruling* us. Now that I know your father is *helping* Russia rule us, well—" I stopped. I had no idea where to go with that. "It's just—interesting."

I would later learn that there was a reason I wasn't aware of Russia's ruling hand on Finland: until right around that time in the mid-nineties it had been extraordinarily light. The official position had all along been that Finland was an independent nation with its own constitution but with some minimal Russian oversight. That light hand had been aggravating Russia's patriotic reactionaries, though, more and more, for some years already. They had been insisting that Finland was a Russian *province*, not an independent nation, and demanding that the Tsar crack the whip, that he and his noble henchmen kick and pummel us into pan-Slavic submission. To make us Russian, russify us. We knew nothing about that back then.

We also didn't know that the Tsar was already beginning to yield to the fearful forces of reaction. The iron fist was in our near future. For now, for me, the Russian military presence just around the corner from where I was standing at that moment was just—interesting.

In the summer of 1895 I was still very young. I was nineteen, months away from twenty. I was also a crofter's kid who had been invited to mingle with a higher class of people, people who seemed not only older and richer but more cultivated, more worldly.

And yet they didn't despise me. After breakfast, in fact, they asked me where I was staying, and when I described my living situation, they asked if I would like to move in with them. I did, of course, and was too young and too earnest to hide my feelings. I just blurted them out. Maiju and M just smiled.

By lunch I had walked to my mother's cousin's place in Rööperi and gotten my things, thanked my host and said I was moving out. He was relieved, as I expected; but there was some other kind of reaction mixed in with the relief, and I couldn't make out its features. Fear of exposure? Sullen self-protection? Who knew? I didn't need to care.

And so a new phase of my life began. I met the twins' mother and father, called the father "Your Honor." He smiled indulgently over at his twins, then told me I should save the formal address for public occasions, and call him Mr. Lassila in private.

5

It was maybe two years later, one spring day when M was out, that Maiju came up to me and kissed me. On the lips. For a long time. Maybe a minute. I didn't know what to think. I could feel my eyes flicking back and forth like a bird in a cage. We had lived together for two years without any of that nonsense; what was this now?

I didn't pull away, though. I thought Maiju probably knew what ta was doing, and would explain it to me when ta was done.

Finally ta did pull away. Ta looked at me quizzically.

"You didn't enjoy that, did you?"

I shrugged. "I didn't *hate* it."

"But you haven't been wanting to kiss me."

I'm not sure what my face did, but whatever it was, it made ta laugh.

"No," ta nodded with a smile. "You aren't physically attracted to me."

"I am too!" I protested.

"But—?"

I blushed. Unfortunately, I do that a lot.

"I—" I began. "I've always found you and M exciting. Physically exciting. That's why I came backstage to meet you."

"Okay," Maiju nodded. "I see what you mean. Let me rephrase that: you aren't sexually attracted to me."

"I, um—I don't exactly know what that means," I said lamely.

"Hm," ta said. "Okay, let me put it this way. Has there ever been anyone you've wanted to kiss the way I kissed you?"

"No. Should there be?"

Maiju smiled. "No. Most people, yes. Most people have sexual attractions. You don't. And that's fine. Because I don't either. And M doesn't. The three of us, we're different."

"But why?"

"I don't know. We just are."

"I mean, but why did you kiss me?"

"Oh, that. I was just testing a theory."

"About me?"

"About us. All three of us."

"I see. And the test confirmed your theory?"

"Yes."

"And your conclusion is? Your, what is it called—your *finding*?"

Maiju laughed again. "My *finding*," ta said, "is that you and I are soulmates."

"I don't know that word," I said.

"It means we fit together perfectly."

"Oh," I said. "That's good, then. I agree with your finding!"

Maiju smiled and put an arm around my shoulders. "I agree too," ta said. Then thought of something: "Does this arm bother you?"

"No," I said, and put my arm around ta's shoulders. "Does this arm bother you?"

Ta shook ta's head and we both smiled. And that was that. Till the day ta died.

6

Two literary observations to make at this point.

The first is that Maiju's eighth novel, one of the seven (*seven!*) ta published in 1912, the ostensibly autobiographical *Rakkautta* ("Love"), is not really autobiographical. It's not the memoir it seems to be. It is one in the fairly superficial sense that the "Maiju Lassila" narrator lives in Tohmajärvi, where Maiju and M were indeed born and raised, and the narrator's father is the local *vallesmanni* or sheriff, which their father was; but the love story that drives the plot of that novel, or what the novel pretends is or was a love story, never happened. There was no rich Petteri. And Maiju was never a "girl" who was interested in "boys." But then the novel is actually quite tricky. It's not really a love story. It's more of an anti-love story. It's a pastiche, a parody of love stories. The Maiju Lassila who narrates that novel shows her younger female self pretending to be in love with the rich boy, to all appearances because she was interested in his money, but actually because her author wanted to make fun of love stories.

The second is that an hour or two after the kissing scene I began to feel like I was inside Maiju's head. Or perhaps ta's body. Telepathy, I suppose you'd call it; but to put it in literary terms (remember: "textually" attracted), I began to feel like a close third-person narrator. I knew what ta was thinking, feeling, experiencing. And Maiju felt me the same way. Together or apart, from across the room or from across town, we felt each other. Like lovers without sex. Or rather, perhaps, like shared selves, manifold selves shared in both bodies. I gradually became convinced, in fact, that I contained shoreless swarms of adoptive identities, and so did Maiju and M. I walked about inside their collective identities and they walked about in mine—though I had more restricted access to M's embodied manifold. [21] I suspect ta

---

[21] This paragraph is perhaps the premier passage where, according to the ever-truculent Prof. Julius Nyrkki, several of my phrasings in English resonate "suspiciously" with similar phrasings in Giovanni Pontiero's English translation of José Saramago's *The Year of the Death of Ricardo Reis*—suggesting, according to him, that I am not so much translating a "nonexistent" Finnish original as adapting Pontiero.

Pontiero's recurring phrases, however, are "innumerable beings/people," "multiple," and "multitudes"; and while the *image* of internal multiplicity is similar in the two novels, my phrasings do not borrow from Pontiero. What I translate there as "shared selves, manifold selves shared in both bodies" in "Vatanen's" Finnish is *jaettuja miniä, moninaisia kummassakin kehossa yhteisiä miniä* (lit. "shared I's, multitudinous in both bodies common/shared I's"). "I contained shoreless swarms of identities" in Finnish is *minussa oli rannaton suure henkilöllisyyksien parvia* (lit. "in me was a shoreless quantity of identity swarms"). "I walked about inside their collective identities" in Finnish is *Kuljeskelin heidän joukkohenkilöllisyyksissään* (lit. "I wandered in their group identities"). And, finally, "embodied manifold" in Finnish is *ruumiillistunut useus* (lit. "embodied manyness"), in the illative case (*pääsy johonkin* "access to something").

One further note: *kummassakin kehossa* "in both bodies" is a telling phrase, because the Finnish word *keho* "body" was not coined until 1945, by the Finnish linguist Hannes Teppo, on the model of Estonian *keha* "body"—suggestive evidence that this novel cannot have been written in the early 1920s. The older Finnish word for body, *ruumis*, which is featured in *ruumiillistunut* "embodied," had come to mean a *dead* body or corpse, necessitating a new word denoting a living body. *Ruumiillistuma* "embodiment" likewise still means a living or metaphorical incarnation (it can also mean an epitome or quintessence); as we'll see in Chapter 20 of the "After" section of the novel, Algot Untola's ectoplasmic body is described as the apparently living (but perhaps metaphorical) *ruumiillistuma* "embodiment" or "incarnation" of his spirit or soul. [Tr.]

protected ta's clandestine work that way. I never asked.

What happened that first time was that I was sitting on the sofa with the book of Shakespeare's *Tempest* in English, watching in my mind's eye as the hound-shaped goblins chased Caliban, Trinculo, and Stephano into the swamps, when I thought I heard Maiju suggest that we go for a walk. I looked over at the dining room table, where ta was apparently reading the newspaper, not looking at me. Puzzled, I began "Did you just ..." and without turning ta's head toward me ta gave a sly smile—and I *knew*, not only that ta was smiling, though I could not see ta's face, but that ta had thought the suggestion, not voiced it. So I took it inward: *Did you just ...*, and ta nodded slightly, eyes still on the paper. *Sure*, I thought then, *let's go for a walk*. And ta turned in ta's chair to face me full on, put ta's hands on ta's knees, and said out loud, with that peculiar Maiju light in ta's eyes, "Well it's about time!" And I felt a rush of warmth—the warmth of love. The warmth of life.

So we went for that walk, gloved hand in gloved hand. It was a chilly spring day in late March, so we bundled up, but the sun was shining brightly and there was almost no snow along the roadway. In our warm trousers and jackets we looked like two men walking along holding hands, and I worried what people would say, but Maiju dismissed my worries calmly. *Let them think and say what they want. That's their problem, not ours.* Hearing my unspoken reply, ta laughed: *What, you're afraid of a little scuffle with insecure boys?*

Outside the apartment building's front door we turned right on Laivastokatu and walked along the shore, looking out at the warships anchored in North Harbor, and at the islands behind them across the water—and Maiju started quizzing me telepathically.

What's that one called?

I don't know.

Tervasaari ("Tar Island"). *How about that one?*

I don't know.
Sompasaari ("Ring Island").
And that next one?
Isn't that—Korkeasaari ("High Island")*?*
Right. And what did they build there a few years ago?
A zoo.
Right.

We took the lower road, closer to the shore. There were a few riders on the road, and a horse-drawn workers' cart clip-clopped past, hauling building materials. The upper road, also part of Laivastokatu, began to rise, a meter, two meters, three meters (the metric system already feeling like second nature to us[22]), and then turned sharp right up away from the water. The lower road took us past ramshackle warehouses and loading docks, where burly dockworkers were bustling about loading and unloading. The air in front of one warehouse was saturated with the pungent smell of coffee beans, from the sacks being hauled up on men's shoulders from the cargo ship tied up at the pier below and loaded into a horse-drawn truck. Now that the waterways were again free of ice after the long winter, ships were bringing us the world again.

Soon the road opened up to the Marine Barracks, where Maiju's father worked, large classical buildings painted yellow. We didn't go in physically, but Maiju took me on a quick tour in ta's memory, opening doors, walking down long halls, up stairs, more halls, knocking on a door, ta's father opening, smiling to see us—or, well, to see Maiju.

Past the Barracks the road veered around to the right and became Katajanokanranta, the Katajanokka Shore road, the Juniper Beak Shore road. The sea was wider at this point, looking east, until we came around to the south shore and could see another big island.

---

[22] The metric system was introduced in Finland between 1886 and 1892, several years before this 1897 walk. [Tr.]

Which is called what? Maiju asked.

Viapori.

Which is the Finnish pronunciation of what Swedish name?

I don't know.

Sveaborg.

Oh.

What is it?

A fortress of some sort. A sea fortress built by the Swedes.

Built when?

I don't know, the 1600s?

The 1740s. Why?

To protect Helsinki against attack.

From?

The Russians, presumably.

Right. But the Swedes also kept a whole fleet there, and infantry troops, to mobilize against a Russian attack anywhere. Stockholm was just too far away.

But it didn't work, did it?

No, it didn't. When did the Russians take Finland?

1809.

Right. In 1808 they occupied Helsinki with their infantry and cavalry, but for months they had to lay siege to Viapori, which they reached in the winter, over the ice.

We didn't know then what a dire role Viapori—or Suomenlinna ("Finland's Fortress"), as we began to call it after the Civil War—would play in future events. The deaths by starvation and disease of thousands of Red prisoners of war. The execution of the twins' friend Algot Untola.

We kept walking along the southern shore, past more brick warehouses and loading docks on the left and wooden dwellings on the right, then turned right on Satamakatu ("Port Road") to Kanavakatu ("Canal Street") and walked through Katajanokka Park to Rahapajankatu ("Mint Street"), past the

Mint,[23] then around Uspensky Cathedral. Coming down the hill from the cathedral we skirted the train yard, where we saw the usual row of old men sitting on a low brick wall up against the bottom of the hill, with the cathedral looming high above their heads behind them. They were former stevedores, working-class men, rough men, the kind of men I had grown up around and felt very comfortable with; they looked, though, like chickens perched on a fence. They grumbled to their neighbors in low voices; one half-stood to ruffle his feathers against the cold, then settled himself back down with the others.

Crossing the tracks, we continued on to the northern shore, where we picked up Kanavakatu again and turned right toward Laivastokatu and home.

In the apartment an odd thing happened. On the dining table there was a note from M. He had paid a quick visit while we were out, had scribbled "All's well, sorry to miss you, M."

What was odd about that? Well, several things.

One was that I saw M. I felt ta, from the inside out, but also saw ta sitting there. Ta looked up, as if aware of me as well, but "said" nothing. I couldn't see where ta was sitting. At first I thought ta was in the room with us, sitting at the table. But when I blinked, ta was gone.

Another was that Maiju apparently couldn't connect with ta's twin. Maiju surged with mixed emotions: equally sorry to miss M and irritated and frustrated at M's refusal to sit for a while to wait for us. Ta stomped around for a minute or two, shaking ta's arms in the air, flashing annoyed eyes.

The third and oddest thing was that in this reality we found in the apartment M was mostly no longer living there. Somehow it was three or four years later and M had all but

---

[23] The Mint of Finland was opened on Katajanokka in 1864, the year the Finnish mark was established as the official currency of the Grand Duchy of Finland. It continued to operate in that location until 1988, when it moved to Vantaa. [Tr.]

moved out, appearing only very briefly and unpredictably. And somehow I *knew* that it was 1900 or 1901—for a few minutes. Then it was 1897 again.

In literary terms, it was a flash-forward.[24]

Maiju and I didn't talk about it. Ta just stopped and looked over and we held each other's gaze for a second or two. That was enough.

---

[24] "Vatanen's" Finnish for flash-forward here is *pikakelaus,* which is literally a *fast*-forward on a reel-to-reel tape recorder—though in fact reel-to-reel audio tape recording wasn't invented until 1928, six years after the supposed writing of this memoir-novel. [Tr.]

7

That was the year that Maiju took up photography. It was of course an upper-class hobby, but then Maiju was an upper-class kind of person. I was intrigued one day to see a strange leather box under ta's arm as ta sidled in through the front door. It was, ta said, a camera. An Adlake drop plate magazine camera, to be specific—though of course that meant nothing to me. Apparently, instead of a tripod and a long exposure time (whatever those things were), this camera had a mechanical shutter and could take photographs very quickly. It came with twelve plates that you could expose and then store until you were ready to develop the pictures you had taken.

Develop?

Turn the images on the plates into photographs.

How?

In the dark.

Dark?

I'm going to need to have a darkroom built.

I had no idea what a darkroom was, of course, but I was to find out in the next few weeks. Maiju hired a contractor to come in and turn one windowless corner of the large apartment into a little room that could be made perfectly dark. It had a special ruby light for working on the photos, with red fabric wrapped around it, and a table with some pans on it, and a large processing apparatus called an enlarger.

Do you know how to use all this? I asked.

Not yet. But a friend is coming over to teach me.

The friend was actually a Russian colleague of the twins' father, Ivan Aleksandrovich Timiryazev. [25] He was maybe fifteen or twenty years older than us, and had moved to Helsinki to serve as the Governor-General's adjutant several years before. And he was an amateur photographer who wandered around Helsinki in his free time taking photographs of ordinary people and places—many of which had already been published, in magazines like *Veckans Krönika* ("Chronicle of the Week") and *Suomen Kuvalehti* ("Finland's Picture Magazine"). Unlike most of the Russian officers in Finland, he had gone to the trouble to learn Finnish. He was a big friendly chatty man with a heavy Russian accent.

---

[25] Ivan Timiryazev (1860-1927) served as adjutant to the Russian Governor-General of Finland from his arrival from Russia in 1890 till his retirement in 1917—which was, of course, also the end of the Governor-General's lordship over the Finnish Grand Duchy, as independence was declared by the Finns and recognized by Russia that year. Timiryazev, in other words, served in a very high position throughout the years of oppression (1899-1917)—even the worst ones, Bobrikov's Governor-Generalship from 1898 to his assassination in 1904. Timiryazev did spend the rest of his life in Finland, though; he married a Finnish woman named Onerva Angervo in 1918 at the age of 58 and lived with her until his death nine years later.

His photographs of Helsinki are universally admired. Many of them are on display in the Helsinki City Museum. In fact several of the photographs attributed by the pseudonymous author of this novel to Maiju Lassila sound suspiciously like ones attributed to Timiryazev in the museum: the photo of trash in the marketplace after the booths have been cleared away; the picture of the telegram boys lined up in 1914, ready to run telegrams from the war; the long August 1917 food line due to shortages caused by the First World War; the line for potatoes in the marketplace in 1918; the kids chatting with a mounted German soldier standing guard in 1918; and the exploded wreck of a Russian torpedo boat in 1918. Whoever this author was, it is likely that s/he paid a visit to the Helsinki City Museum and "borrowed" credit for those photos in order to give it to Maiju. [Tr.]

He *liked* it here. He wanted to stay in Finland.

Maiju had met Ivan Aleksandrovich on a visit to ta's father's office; when the father introduced him as the Governor-General's adjutant and a noted photographer, Maiju's ears had perked up. They had talked over coffee. When Maiju had expressed a desire to take photographs as well, Ivan Aleksandrovich had promised to teach ta the basics. He paid us a visit, demonstrated how to develop the exposures Maiju had taken on the first baryta-coated glass plate. The next time Maiju did it all alone. The third time, ta invited me along.

It was like magic. Like alchemy. The red light, the acrid smell of the chemicals, the sliding enlarger apparatus: I half-expected the pans to produce bright gold nuggets.

So it was that early one chill morning a few weeks later, Maiju left carrying the leather camera box under one arm. I stayed home, but rode along just behind ta's eyes in spirit.

Where are you headed? I asked.

I have an idea, was all ta would say.

What idea?

You'll see.

I shrugged. I would indeed see. I would follow and see with—well, I was going to say my own eyes. But I'm not sure whose eyes I was seeing with.

Maiju headed into the center. Turned onto Kanavakatu, crossed the middle bridge onto the mainland, and turned left on North Esplanade, the street running along the north side of the long skinny park called the Esplanade.

If you are not from Helsinki, you may be surprised to learn that there is also a street running along the park to the south, called the South Esplanade.

Sorry, that's a lame joke.

After Market Square, Maiju cut over onto the path running down the middle of the park—the wide path where all the beautiful people went to be seen. I thought perhaps ta was headed for Restaurant Kappeli, but instead ta followed the central path west. I had heard the French word *flaneurs* used to describe certain flamboyant young men walking there— *flanöörit* in Finnish—a word whose meaning I never quite understood.

Today, though, the snow was crisp on the path. Almost no one was out.

At the west end of the Esplanade, which in Finnish we called Espa, the path emptied straight into the Swedish Theater, Svenska Teatern. When I'd been in school it had been called Nya Theatern, the New Theater; they'd changed the name around the time I was finishing my studies. It was the Swedish Theater; Maiju and M worked for the Finnish Theater. No real symmetry there, though, because the Swedish Theater was much older, a half century older. Swedish had of course been the colonial language for six hundred years. The elite still mostly spoke Swedish. So of course the Swedish Theater came first.

Maiju walked straight in through the front doors and headed for the stairs. Up and up we climbed—Maiju breathing a little harder, I floating up effortlessly. Up to the fifth floor. Maiju searched out a door with a plate on it announcing TILL TAKET: "to the roof." Oh.

And up we climbed until a door opened onto a catwalk. Maiju walked around to the right till ta was looking east, back over the snowy stretch of the Esplanade—Espa.

Beautiful, I thought.

See?

Looking out over it, I thought Espa was completely deserted. But when I saw the photo Maiju had taken from up there, I spotted a single pedestrian on the path, looking like a black ant from up on that catwalk. The pedestrian was in the western section, called the Theater Esplanade. In the middle section, the Runeberg Esplanade, stood the statue of J L

Runeberg,[26] facing away from us. The eastern section, the Kappeli Esplanade, could just barely be made out in the photo. Maiju pointed out to me, as we studied that photo, how ta had not shot straight up the middle path. Ta had shot at a slightly oblique angle from a spot to the right of center. Makes it more dynamic, ta thought. Something ta had learned from talking to Ivan.

Up on the catwalk, though, there were no photography lessons.

Step back a little, was the only advice ta directed my way. *Stop crowding me.*

I didn't realize I was standing anywhere, I protested.

Some ghost you are, ta grumbled. But affectionately.

---

[26] Johan Ludvig Runeberg (1804-1877) was the greatest Finnish poet of the nineteenth century, often called Finland's national poet. He wrote in Swedish, and wielded a strong influence over nineteenth-century poetry in Sweden as well. He was a National Romantic who gave Finns an idealized literary identity, especially in *The Tales of Ensign Stål* (1848-1860), about the Finnish War in 1808-1809, in which the Russians annexed Finland from Sweden. Nothing personal, but Runeberg's Romantic idealism powered the repressive respectability that inspired August Ahlqvist to vilify Aleksis Kivi and his great 1870 novel (see note 10 on p. 5). This scene with Maiju photographing the snowy landscape looking east over the Esplanade, toward the Runeberg statue, is a very Runebergian one, Romantically soft and pure; but Ahlqvist would have hated this novel, especially the "After" second half, almost as much as he hated Kivi's. (Kivi's *Brothers Seven* too had passages of soft Romantic purity; see e.g. the tale Aapo tells of the Pale Maiden, on pp. 143-48 of my *The Brothers Seven*.) [Tr.]

8

One rather momentous thing that happened in those years toward the end of the century was that the Aspegrens split up and their theater split in two as well. One part headed out into the provinces to tour, under the name The New Theater; Mr. Aspegren kept the other splinter going, somehow, in Helsinki, for another two years. By 1898 I was seeing the writing on the wall, and started looking around for another theater. Maiju put in a good word for me with Kaarlo Bergbom and his sister Emilie, but they said they had no vacancies. I held on at the Finnish People's Theater for another eight months—it was, after all, my first real home, and I felt a strong bond of loyalty to Mr. Aspegren—but things just kept getting worse. And when they started talking about becoming a provincial touring company also, maybe merging with The New Theater again, I quit.

I didn't want to leave Helsinki. I didn't want to leave the twins.

What to do? I didn't have a job to go to. Maiju and M assured me that I could stay with them as long as I liked, rent-free. I had never paid rent anyway, so nothing changed, except that I was home a lot more. I started trying to write a novel—beginning with a fictionalized autobiography, as so many novelists do, and tearing up partial draft after partial draft. Those drafts would eventually turn into *The Helpless Ones*, but I had to learn a lot about novel-writing before that could happen.

I also needed to learn about myself, truth be told. I tended to move through life as if in a dream. I didn't have enough substance, it seemed to me, to flesh out a novel—especially an autobiographical one!

I went on long walks through the city, and in the long dark winter months trudged for hours across the frozen harbors around Katajanokka. Sometimes Maiju and I would go skiing. Two or three times a winter the twins would take me ice-skating on a rink created on the ice over in front of Uspensky Cathedral. The winters were warmer and wetter here in Helsinki than they'd been back home in Ostrobothnia, but still cold enough to freeze the harbor waters. And we were far enough south that we had a good six hours of sun every day, instead of the four we'd had back home. Summers we had the same six hours of dark every night. It wouldn't start getting light until three or so in the morning.

Some afternoons I would walk with Maiju and M to the theater, just to have their company for another half hour before they disappeared into work for the day. Our conversations as we walked ranged widely, from literature and drama to religion to politics to science and technology.

One day in August of the century's last year we saw our first motorcar in the Helsinki streets. All along the roadway people stopped to gawk and comment. The voices around us were sure that it was driven by a Russian aristocrat, who had presumably motored over from St. Petersburg; they argued over whether it was Count This or Prince That. Someone else knew that it was a Mercedes Simplex. It was blue, with gold wheels. It was interesting, I guess, but gaudy. Ostentatious. Its message to me, to all of us, was clear: *look what I have and you don't*. A few days later in the paper there was an advertisement for Patria and Phoebus motorcars—which actually looked like motorbikes that had been given two extra wheels each.

One day, also, as we were walking through Market Square

just across the bridge from Katajanokka, I asked the twins whether they minded stopping for a moment while I bought myself a rye loaf to munch on while I worked on my novel that day. Maiju and M gaped at me aghast.

"You're going to buy bread *here*? In the *market*?"

I was too surprised to feel ashamed. The shame would crawl through me later.

"I—I've always bought bread at the market," I stammered. "They have special bakery stalls."

"Of course they do," Maiju said—a bit condescendingly, I thought. "But let us show you where to buy *good* bread."

And they took me to the Ekberg bakery on Aleksanterin-katu. It was a three-story brick building. You could get coffee and tea there as well. They asked me what I wanted, and I was about to say a *limppu*, a round rye loaf, but then I saw the pole stretched above the man's head with delicious-looking *reikä-leipä* ("hole bread") loaves strung onto it—thinner and crunch-ier rye loaves with a hole in the middle, precisely so they could be stored on a horizontal pole like that—and asked for one of them instead. It was still warm in my hands. As we walked out of the store Maiju encouraged me to tear off a piece and try it. I did. It was, frankly, glorious. It had a kind of crispy surface, underneath which the dark rye pulsed with flavor. It filled my mouth with my home in heaven—the closest I would ever get to that home, in which I didn't believe.

Maiju smiled at the expression on my face.

"See?"

I nodded. On that day Ekberg became my regular destina-tion. I would walk with Maiju and M and say goodbye to them at Ekberg Café. I had my notebook in my bag, and would sit at a table trying to write my novel for hours, nursing a cup of coffee and one of their smaller "rye pieces."[27] I ran a tab. Every

---

[27] This is a telling anachronism: so-called rye pieces (*ruispalat*) were first introduced in 1974—suggesting that the actual author of *The Last Days of Maiju Lassila* is our contemporary. [Tr.]

few weeks Maiju or M would casually pay it, without comment.

On New Year's and New Century's Day, 1900—the twins' 27th birthday—the Bergboms told the cast and staff at the Finnish Theater that they would be building a new theater on Railway Square, and that the theater's name would change with the christening of the new building, to the Finnish National Theater. I still didn't have a job. Mysteriously, though, saying nothing of ta's plans to either Maiju or me, M decided to quit the theater soon after the announcement, and Maiju dragged me in to meet the Bergboms, had me audition for M's place on staff, with a monologue from *Richard III*—"Was ever woman in this humor wooed?"[28] Maiju picked the monologue; I did the tyrant's insecurity with his "dissembling looks" as best I could; and the Bergboms hired me. I wasn't sure I liked the nationalistic ring of the theater's new name, but after the Swedish it was Finland's premier theater, and when we got to tour the new building, a few weeks before the opening in the spring of 1902, I was impressed in spite of myself. It was a bit grandiose, of course. Ida Aalberg said it looked like the Bolshoi in Moscow; Bruno Böök, who had played Aalberg's leading man so many times audiences thought they were a couple offstage as well, said it looked more like the Theater an der Wien in Vienna. I had never been in either city, but it seemed to me to look more like the Swedish Theater. I'd never seen a play performed at the Swedish, but had visited it spectrally with Maiju that time, on ta's photography outing. I didn't say so out loud, but in my head I was also thinking that it made the audience feel like they were in the Golden Mansions of Heaven.

My parents and grandparents and aunts and uncles were

---

[28] Paavo Cajander (1846-1913) was the first to translate the complete works of Shakespeare into Finnish, and his translations have stood the test of time. His translation of *Richard III* was published in 1897, three years before this audition. [Tr.]

fervent followers of Paavo Ruotsalainen's Pietist revival movement, the Awakening.[29] Me, I'd never had much use for that
religious stuff. But, you know, I'm only human. I walk into the
National Theater's new building for the first time, I'm as
susceptible to that kind of mansions-of-heaven impression as
the next person.

And of course a job is a job.

There were other benefits, too. After a show we'd all
traipse over to Esplanade Park, Espa, and crowd into Restaurant Kappeli—called that, Maiju told me, because it looked on
the outside like a chapel. It was where Helsinki's art elite hung
out. Our entourage was always welcome: the National Theater! Our big stars would greet Eino Leino and Juhani Aho, Jean
Sibelius and Oskar Merikanto, Akseli Gallen-Kallela, many
others.[30] Sometimes they would invite us to their tables, push

---

[29] Paavo Ruotsalainen (1777-1852) was the most prominent and charis-
matic leader of the Awakening (*herännäisyys* or *körttiläisyys* in Finnish)—
not its founder. The revival movement arose out of ecstatic experiences
various people had in the late eighteenth century, falling into trances and
babbling in hay fields, for example; Paavo Ruotsalainen emerged as its
leader in the 1820s, and traveled all over Finland preaching the revivalist
gospel, mostly on foot. The movement spread so fast that, even though it
remained within the Evangelical Lutheran Church of Finland, the ecclesias-
tical authorities grew concerned, and put Ruotsalainen on trial in 1838. He
was convicted and fined in 1839, but that had no diminishing effect on the
movement. [Tr.]

[30] Eino Leino (1878-1926) was a neo-Romantic poet who also translated
classics (notably Dante's *Divine Comedy*) and wrote novels. He was probably Finland's premier poet at the turn of the century and until his early
death of neurosyphilis (specifically, *tabes dorsalis*) at the age of 47. We will
meet him again later in the novel. Juhani Aho (1861-1921) was a realistic
novelist; we'll see him reviewing the National Theater's production of a
Plautus play below (p. 65). Jean Sibelius (1865-1957) and Oskar Merikanto
(1868-1924) were then and still are today two of Finland's most beloved
composers; Akseli Gallen-Kallela (1865-1931) was one of Finland's greatest
painters. [Tr.]

tables and chairs around, create a whole island of artists; other times they would nod briefly and continue their private confabulations. No matter: we had our own. Or the others did: I was mostly a silent observer. Maiju would sometimes get drawn into a heated debate on this or that play or political event, but often ta sat silently as I did, surveying the scene, registering the voices and the gestures. We would eat and drink, often whole meals with beer or wine, sometimes just coffee or tea and a pastry. One night Maiju decided to give me a tour of the wall paintings: the splotchy thoughtful face of Gambrinus, the legendary inventor of beer, painted on the round wall medallion in the kitchen by Albert Edelfelt; the moody Rouen street scene painted on the kitchen wall by Oscar Kleineh; the sunny sea scene splashed across one wall of the bar by Hjalmar Munsterhjelm.[31] The restaurant had been a gathering place for artists since the middle of the last century; Maiju said those artists had painted those paintings as thanks, two or three decades before. There was also a remarkable Helsinki panorama in the Kappeli Cellar, but Maiju had no idea who had painted it.

This was also the time when, in addition to quitting the theater, M started staying away from home for months at a stretch. At first I didn't make the connection with that experience at the end of our spring walk two years before, when Maiju and I had seemingly jumped ahead in time. It was a few days before that light burned on. Maiju was there when I realized. Again we just exchanged looks. Maiju nodded.

What's M doing? was all I asked.

Ta shrugged: *Spying.*

Spying?

Ta nodded.

---

[31] Albert Edelfelt (1854-1905), Oscar Kleineh (1846-1919), and Hjalmar Munsterhjelm (1840-1905) were an older generation of Finnish painters; they painted their wall paintings in Kappeli in the late 1870s. [Tr.]

I thought about it. This was another new idea to me.

"Is that like finding things out?" I asked aloud. "Without other people knowing about it?"

Sounds like a reasonable guess, Maiju thought.

Spying on the Russians? I thought. *Or for them?*

I don't know, ta replied. *M wouldn't tell me.*

It was also around that time, shortly after the turn of the century, that I got to know Algot Untola, the Lassilas' friend from back in Tohmajärvi. He had been working for several years as a teacher in tiny coastal towns in Ostrobothnia, farther north than where I grew up, and in 1893 had taken up a teaching job in Viipuri;[32] when he knocked on our door in Katajanokka he was moving to St. Petersburg, where among other things he would be selling lumber. He'd made a trip over from Viipuri to pick up some things before heading down to the Russian capital. He was a small wiry man with a scraggly goatee and pince-nez glasses.

---

[32] Viipuri is the Finnish pronunciation and spelling of Vyborg, the castle built by the Swedes in the late thirteenth century and the town that grew up around it, in Karelia, a Finno-Ugric culture in the borderland between Finland and Russia. The Swedes and Russians fought over it for centuries, but the Swedes controlled it until Peter the Great captured it in 1710; the rest of Finland, including Viipuri/Vyborg and the west-Karelian Isthmus around it, was ceded to Russia in the 1809 Treaty of Hamina. When Finland gained its independence from Russia in 1917, the old borders of the Grand Duchy were maintained, and western Karelia remained with Finland; eastern Karelia (then called Soviet Karelia) rose up against the Soviet Union and sought to be united with Finland in the late teens and early twenties, but the various rebellions were expeditiously crushed. 30,000 east-Karelian refugees then fled across the border into Finland. Viipuri and western Karelia were captured by the Soviets in the Winter War of 1939-1940, and then first retaken and then lost again by the Finnish-German alliance in the 1941-1944 Continuation War; this time 400,000 west-Karelian refugees fled across the border into Finland. Finns still think of Viipuri as basically theirs, and grieve that it's locked away outside their eastern border. [Tr.]

Looking back on that meeting, and remembering the rather intense but ultimately harmless man-child in his early thirties that he was then, I wonder where the signs were that this was a person who would be viciously murdered by the new state authorities just eighteen years later.

9

The first sign that trouble lay ahead came in February, 1899, when Tsar Nikolai II signed a bill into law that seemed to everybody to be saying that Finns no longer had any say over what happened in our country. Russia now had all the power.

The word I heard people using for it was "coup."[33] I didn't know that word, or understand the politics of it—the legal terms and their implications. I mainly had a vague image in my head, of a bully pushing a smaller kid off his bike and saying, "This is mine now." What confused me was this other sense I had that we were already Russia's bike—that Russia had been riding its Finnish bicycle for 90 years. Hadn't they always had all the power?

I thought back to me telling Maiju, just four years earlier, that Russia was more "interesting" to me now that I knew that the twins' father was helping the Russians rule us. What naïveté! What did I understand about any of it? Nothing. Not one thing.

I asked Maiju. Ta was as confused as I was. Our colleagues

---

[33] The word "Vatanen" uses for "coup" in Finnish is *valtionkaappaus*, which is literally something like "state-grabbing" (or "state-(hi)jacking"). The big question historically was whether Finland was an independent state that Russia annexed or a Russian province that had been given far too much autonomy for its own good. The former had been the assumption on both sides of the border since 1809; the latter had increasingly been the assumption of Russian reactionaries since the 1870s. [Tr.]

at the theater didn't know either. Everybody was half-angry, half-panicky—but wholly bewildered. What the hell was going on? What did this mean for us?

When the "coup" happened, M disappeared for three weeks. When ta reemerged in early March it was morning and Maiju and I were home. We rushed to the entry hall and asked ta what ta knew; ta said, "Not here. Let's go skiing. Pack a lunch."

So we busied ourselves in the kitchen, made six sandwiches on Ekberg's dark rye bread and wrapped them in wax paper, boiled some eggs, packed a bottle of red wine and some sturdy glasses, loaded the lunch into canvas rucksacks, then laced up our ski boots, grabbed our skis and poles, and headed out the door and down the stairs.

None of us broke the silence as we crossed the road and stopped to step into our skis. No one spoke as we skied across North Harbor. At first it seemed M was taking us to Korkeasaari, but no: once we got past the Marine Barracks pier ta turned us right, to the east. Hylkysaari ("Wreck Island"), the tiny island nestled up close to the eastern shore of Korkeasaari, maybe? No: that had buildings on it. The shipyard looked defunct, and the villas were presumably designed for summer use only—but we saw a man coming out of the front door of one with a rug, hanging it on the rug-beating rack, and clobbering great clouds of dust out of it with a wicker beater. We kept skiing.

Soon it became clear that M was guiding us to an even tinier island farther out in the harbor. It took us a good hour to ski to it. But the weather was perfect for skiing. Over to our right the late-winter sun climbed lazily about halfway up into the morning sky, warmed us a little. The *swoosh swoosh* of our skis was calming. I began to feel everything was going to be okay. M was on the job. Ta would explain everything, and life would go on as before.

When we got to the island—M said it was called Nimismies, which was the name of their father's job in Tohmajärvi: the official title for *vallesmanni*, "sheriff"—we undid our skis and wove our way through the trees to the middle of the island, where we found three good sitting rocks and made ourselves at home. Maiju and I passed around the sandwiches; M opened and poured the wine.

"Okay," Maiju said, once we had all eaten one sandwich and washed it down with a few swallows of wine. "So tell us, what's going on?"

"A lot," M said. "Everything is changing for Finland."

"Everything?"

"Well, not quite everything. But legally, politically, yes. Everything important."

"So what is this coup we keep hearing about?"

"A coup, or what the French call a *coup d'état*, a blow to the state, is an overthrow. The Russians have overthrown our government, taken over."

"But what does that mean?" Maiju said. "I mean, for us."

"That's not clear yet," M said. "It could mean lots of things, though. They could ban the Finnish language. Make everybody speak Russian."

"No!"

"It's possible. They could mandate that all schooling take place in Russian. They could disband our military. Effectively they have declared our constitution null and void."

"Explain that," Maiju said.

"The constitution drafted back in 1810 or so and signed by Tsar Nikolai I," M said, "gave Finns self-rule over all matters relating to Finland alone. Whenever we were considering a course of action that could affect Russia as well as us, we had to consult with the Russian authorities, but otherwise it was all up to us. That has all now changed. The February Manifest has effectively undone ninety years of autonomy for Finland."

"How?"

"In that document the Tsar assigned the Diet of Finland an exclusively advisory role," M said, "and reserved all decision-making power to the Russian State Council."

"I don't understand any of this," I said. "But can I ask: any idea why they're doing this?"

"Sure," M said. "Good question. It's called Russification."

"Trying to make us Russian," Maiju said.

"Exactly."

"How do you know that's their plan?"

"Because they've been doing it for decades in the Ukraine, White Russia, Poland, and the Baltics. They all used to have the same special status we've enjoyed, but the Russian state started chipping away at that status back in the late sixties. Finland is the only one that has preserved its special status. And reactionaries in Russia hate that. They want us to be a province of Russia, owing fealty only to Russia, speaking only Russian, thinking and feeling only like Russians. Wipe out all traces of Finnish or Estonian or whatever culture."

"That's been happening for *decades*?" Maiju asked.

"Decades," M nodded. "We've had it relatively easy. And that has been driving the reactionaries out of their tiny minds with rage." M took a gulp of wine, swallowed it hard. "In Estonia, Latvia, and Lithuania Russian was made the only official language in 1870. Think about that: *1870*. Almost three decades ago. Those three countries are now Russian provinces. They want the same for Finland."

"But what about our constitution?" Maiju said. "That was signed by the Tsar back then, you said."

"Yes, and ratified over and over by each successive Tsar—until now. Nikolai II has been under incredible pressure from the reactionaries to crack the whip. Release the iron fist. He's been resisting, I'm told, but the forces of reaction are too strong. Now he has yielded on this; there's no reason to think he won't go on yielding. Taking more and more away from us."

"So there's nothing we can do?"

"That remains to be seen," M said, maybe a little grimly. "I'm told the constitutional authorities not only in Finland but Russia too are working on it. The preliminary consensus is that this was an illegal coup. You know, in theory. But of course Russia is an autocracy, so—" M glanced over at me, saw my puzzled look, then smiled and held up a peeled egg, and explained: "Rule by one man. The Russian Tsar is the Russian state. Whatever he decides to do"—ta took a bite out of the egg—"is the law. No such thing as an 'illegal' decision by the Tsar. That's a contradiction in terms. An impossibility."

"What does this mean for our father?" Maiju asked.

"Nothing, yet," M said. "As long as he does or says nothing that questions this new state of affairs, he's not only safe; he's safer than ordinary Finnish citizens."

"Why?"

"Because he's part of the power structure. He'll be expected to help implement the new order. Help Russia Russify us. Advise his Russian superiors on the best way to accomplish that."

"Is he going to be able to do that?" Maiju asked. "I mean, and still sleep at night?"

"Dad's a political animal," M smiled. "He'll survive."

"What about you?"

"What *about* me?"

"What are you going to do?"

"That remains to be seen," M said. Ta smiled again. "I'm a bit of a political animal myself."

Maiju and I returned ta's smile, nodded sagely. I was feeling very grown-up. 23 now. A mature, responsible adult, reflecting on the fate of the country.

It was, of course, an illusion. I was a babe in arms. I still am, two decades later.

"One last thing," Maiju said.

"Yes?"

"Why are we here?"

"Why are we where?"

"Here on this island. Why did you think we couldn't have this discussion at home? Are we in danger there? Should we watch what we say at home? Are there ears listening in?"

"You never know," M said darkly. "Best to play it safe."

And then, sitting there on snow-encrusted granite in the woods on a tiny island in North Harbor, on the very edge of the Gulf of Finland, the easternmost reach of the Baltic, I had another vision—of the future again, it seemed to me. M and a man I didn't know were running through a city street at night, exuding urgency. Both were breathing heavily but neither seemed to be tiring. The man said to M, "Alert the Kagal, we need to—"

And then the vision faded, just as they were splitting up, M turning left, the man turning right, leaving me wondering:

Kagal?

10

As M had predicted, things got worse. At the turn of the century General Aleksei Kuropatkin, the Russian Minister of War, gave a speech that was printed in the Finnish papers and stirred up all manner of hostility:

> After we conquered Finland, throughout the nineteenth century, we turned far too little attention to the internal affairs of this Russian province. The result of that neglect was a place nestled up close to our capital city that hated us and surged with separatist strivings—a place with a small but incredibly stubborn population. It is left for the twentieth century to take up the urgent task of annexing Finland to Russian nationhood.

And, of course, I remarked to Maiju, savoring the spice of political indignation on my tongue, it seemed to them that the best way to do that was to make us hate them even more.

Maiju just smiled. Wanly. At me, I think, mainly. At my foray into political agency.

We weren't activists. Not like M.

Nikolai Ivanovich Bobrikov had arrived in Finland as the new Governor-General in 1898, with a mandate from the Tsar to instill in the local population—by stages!—a sense of just how important it was for Finland's success to achieve the most intimate and perfect union with all true subjects of the Tsar in a shared fatherland. It wasn't until the February Manifest had been released, though, that he upped the ante, became the dictator that everyone came to hate and fear. The Russian gendarmerie had been brought to Finland in 1889, to spy and inform, but they had acted surreptitiously behind the scenes, so most of us had never heard of them; once the February Manifest was in place, Bobrikov expanded and intensified their duties. They were a Russian military force that answered to no Finn. Bobrikov had them bursting into the homes of suspects in the middle of the night, rounding everybody up and sending them off to jail. They required a special new kind of identification documents, and anyone who didn't have those documents went to jail. All manner of supposedly subversive printed matter was now banned—books, magazines, photographs—and the gendarmes would not only burst into homes in the middle of the night but stop trains to search for "smuggled" and otherwise "illicit" documents.

Maiju and I were not disturbed by the gendarmes.

I asked ta once whether M was running some kind of interference for us. Maiju just shrugged.

Still, even though Maiju and I weren't what you might call *knowers*—we didn't go out of our way to gain knowledge of current affairs—it was hard to avoid picking up tidbits. People around us talked. There was a lot of talk. Some of it stuck.

In June 1900 it was decreed that all Finnish postage stamps be discontinued and replaced with Russian stamps by the following January. The Finnish lion must step aside and give the two-headed Russian eagle pride of place.

It was around that time, though, that Eetu Isto painted his famous painting of a young blonde woman being attacked by Russia's double-headed eagle. The painting was called simply "Attack." It was displayed and copied in secret in a villa in Helsinki's Kaivopuisto; the gendarmes, getting word that it was on display, were preparing to storm the villa, but Isto rolled the painting up and escaped through a window, taking the copies with him. He fled to Sweden and then on to Germany, where a good ten thousand more photographic copies were made, along with six print runs of post cards, one set of which had "Attack" written on it in Russian. These were smuggled back into Finland through Sweden, and Isto's painting became one of the best-known symbols of the years of oppression. Hundreds of "Attack" postcards were sent to Finland through the mail, many with black stamps signaling mourning for the country plastered on top of the Russian ones.

Russian itinerant peddlers had been a part of rural Finnish culture for a very long time. Not only did I remember them coming around in my childhood, selling all manner of useful items that they had brought from Russia, but my parents and grandparents remembered the same from their childhoods. Now, though, those peddlers had apparently started spreading rumors among the rural landowners that the Russian authorities were planning to redistribute all the farmland and forestland in Finland to all the crofters.

When I heard those rumors I scoffed: an honest emotional response, born of my crofter upbringing. Why would the royals and aristocrats in St. Petersburg, whose fathers and grandfathers had owned serfs, even consider giving land to poor crofters like my family? But the rumors were stirring up trouble in the heartland, and the Finnish Senate tried to restrict Russian peddlers' rights—until Bobrikov lashed back. He *wanted* trouble in the heartland. Within weeks the Russian Duma had passed a law preventing anyone from limiting Russian citizens' right to earn a living in Finland.

One day in the first summer of the new century, during a break in rehearsals at the theater, a young actor whose name I didn't know started talking about one Vyacheslav Konstantinovich von Plehve, who, this actor said, had been made Actual

Privy Counselor and Finnish Minister Secretary of State the year before. I wasn't the only one present who had never heard the name. Apparently he had come out in full support of abolishing the Finnish Army. I remembered M saying, that day out on the ice, that that was a possible Russification move. In the theater, mutters of disgust from everyone within earshot. Not much more than that.

I didn't hear the name von Plehve for four more years. One day the twins' friend from Tohmajärvi, Algot Untola, knocked on our door, and told us he'd been involved in the conspiracy to assassinate von Plehve, and had had to flee Russia when they succeeded. There'd been a double agent named Yevno Fishelevich Azef, he said, a Jewish revolutionary from White Russia who both organized assassinations for the Socialist Revolutionary Party—called the SRs, pronounced Essers—and worked as a police spy for the Russian secret police. Azef was so angry at von Plehve's tolerance for the bloody wave of anti-Jewish violence that had broken out in 1903 that he accidentally-on-purpose didn't inform on the Essers' plans to assassinate him. Von Plehve managed to survive three attempts on his life before the fatal bomb finally got him.

It seemed Algot had been radicalized in St. Petersburg. Back in Finland, he joined the Finnish revolutionary movement, and lasted another fourteen years until the victorious Whites took him out. So much for the harmless man-boy I'd met four years earlier.

This is my memoir of my life with Maiju; but at some deeper level (which I still don't entirely understand) it is also the story of Algot Untola. I can't say I ever really took to the man. He had annoying mannerisms. He was loud. I think he fancied himself a raconteur. He later wrote novels—one infamously, as we'll see, under the name of Maiju Lassila, which dragged both Maiju and me into his extreme political jeopardy. Maiju claimed to find the novels readable. I couldn't see it.

They seemed stilted and mannered to me. Like the man himself, frankly. Like a wind-up toy banging cymbals.

The last days of a wind-up toy. Sheesh.

M's suggestion out on the ice that they might make us switch from Finnish to Russian also began to prove prophetic in that same summer of 1900. Again, the change was supposed to be gradual: Russian should be adopted as the only official language in several key offices, notably the Governor-General's, and the scope of the change should expand by stages to other offices and departments until Russian was the only official language of the Finnish government. Russian instruction should also be stepped up in schools. This one didn't fare so well. The push-back was massive. In 1902 the so-called Language Manifest was "expanded" and "strengthened" by granting Finnish equal status with Russian in all government offices and courts. Ha.

In the summer of 1901 the Conscription Manifest that von Plehve had supported was ratified by the Finnish Senate. Only four Senators voted against ratification; they were forced to resign their posts. The entire Finnish military wasn't decommissioned immediately, but many departments were; that next winter hundreds of Finnish officers and their families were evicted from their homes, and the corresponding property of the Finnish armed forces—weapons, barracks, movables—was seized without recompense by the Russian Army. The new Russian conscription was slated to begin in 1902, and that would mean the complete decommissioning of the Finnish military.

In the fall of 1901, M later told us, the Kagal was formed—that mysterious word I'd heard in the vision. It was formed as an organization for passive resistance—they disseminated banned books and papers, stirred up resistance to the new conscription law, and generally worked to educate the public—but eventually they grew tired of passive resistance and began to acquire weapons and organize shooting practice. In 1902 they organized a conscription strike. Dozens of Lutheran ministers around the country refused to read the Conscription Manifest to their congregations, and even more congregations were opposed to the readings. In Helsinki only a tiny handful of conscripts obeyed the order; in Ostrobothnia, not one did.

In April of that year a conscription riot broke out in Senate Square at the governmental heart of Helsinki. I was there. It started off as several hundred curious people gathering outside the police station there, and the Russian authorities calling in about twice that many gendarmes. That drew even more Finns to the square. The crowd started heckling the gendarmes, whistling at them, ridiculing them, questioning their masculinity—not that the Russian soldiers understood a word of Finnish, mind—and the cops on horseback tried to silence the crowd with threats. That didn't work. Probably not many in the crowd could understand Russian. So then the authorities called in a hundred Cossacks. That worked. We all scattered. You don't mess around with Cossacks. We didn't go far, though, so we saw how the Cossacks attacked innocent passersby, people just walking through Senate Square, including women and children, lashing out with their sabers and knotted nagaika whips, trampling people with their horses. The rage this awakened in observers was intolerable, and many of them began to intervene, by throwing stones and stabbing Cossacks in the legs with knives.

And then the Cossacks received the order to vacate the square. We later learned that the authorities were worried that the factories would be letting their workers out soon, and if all those people swarmed onto Senate Square the Cossacks would be overrun.

Soon after, the Conscription Manifest was rescinded. No Finns would be conscripted into the Russian army. Instead the Finnish government was forced to pay compensation: twenty million marks.

Bobrikov started exiling leaders of the opposition and firing provincial governors who would not obey him blindly. He started shutting down newspapers that did not toe the line—dozens of them. He decreed that all Finnish street signs must be replaced with signs that displayed the Russian name prominently at the top, with small Finnish and Swedish names beneath. He decreed that all public coachmen—*vossikat* in Finnish, ямщики/*yamschiki* in Russian—must be replaced with Russian citizens.

The man was on a roll.

11

In the 1901-2 season, before we had moved into the new theater building, we put on a production of a Plautus play, *The Clever Slave*.[34] None of us had ever heard of the play or the playwright. Miss Emilie Bergbom, Mr. Bergbom's sister and theater codirector, had learned about it from their father, who taught both her and Kaarlo Latin.[35] Mr. Bergbom, who was directing, told us how she was always the avid language student when they were young; Latin had never stuck to him, and their father had pretty much given up on him in that sphere. He then

---

[34] The play is *Pseudolus*, which Henry Thomas Riley (1816-1878), in the 1852 English translation I use here, titled *Pseudolus, or The Cheat*. The Finnish title Vatanen gives is *Ovela orja*, which I've decided to render slavishly here as *The Clever Slave*, even though the Finnish title has a clever alliteration and assonance to it that the literal English translation lacks. [Tr.]

[35] There is no historical evidence that Emilie Bergbom (1834-1905) ever learned Latin. She spoke Swedish natively and worked with private tutors to learn Finnish, English, and French, all of which she spoke haltingly. Her and Kaarlo's father Gabriel Bergbom (1768-1838) was the Court tax collector (*kruununvouti*) in the Saloinen Hundred, and later, like Maiju and M's father, Court councilor (*hovineuvos*); but there's no evidence that he had any Latin either. Saloinen is a small town on the Gulf of Bothnia coast in northern Ostrobothnia; a Hundred (Finnish *kihlakunta* or *satakunta*, Swedish *härad* or *hundare*) was an administrative division mainly used for taxation purposes, but also for census and the registration of births, deaths, marriages, and so on. [Tr.]

went on to tell the whole story about how she had come to him several months before and suggested they do it, and that she translate it into Finnish for them—the first ever Finnish translation of any Plautus play.[36] Because, he said she had told him, in all kinds of ways it was a play about the theater.

The "clever slave" title character Pseudolus is like a combination playwright and theater director; he not only plots the whole intrigue but tells his master Simo and the audience—the actual audience, in the house—how he is going to trick them, and warns them all not to trust him. Simo in turn warns Ballio, the pimp who is the main target of Pseudolus's deception. And then of course he does successfully trick all of them anyway, despite the fact that they've been warned and are all supposedly on their guard. In fact Pseudolus is constantly attempting to enlist the audience in the house in his design, on the grounds that as a pimp Ballio is the enemy not only of the characters in the play but of the upright members of the audience as well. Over and over Plautus exposes the artifice by which the characters in a play say things "aside" and are supposedly not heard by the other characters standing just a meter or two away: "Why is he talking to himself alone?" Harpax asks the audience once, and similar cases of asides being heard and commented on are frequently used to comic effect. When the young lover Calidorus brings his friend Charinus to Pseudolus to offer his aid, Pseudolus histrionically tells the audience ("aside"!) "I'll address this person in a very lofty strain," and Calidorus's remark on his lofty words is that he is "blustering just like a tragedian." Charinus offers Pseudolus the use of a newly arrived slave in his house named Simmia who is brilliant at deception and disguise, and Pseudolus dresses ta for the role he needs ta to play—impersonating Harpax—and gives ta props and lines.

---

[36] This is a fiction. No play by Plautus has ever been translated or performed in Finland. [Tr.]

There is also some gender play in the piece. The whore that Calidorus is in love with has a grammatically neutered name, Phœnicium; Simmia, who is recruited to pretend to be the macho military man Harpax, has a grammatically feminine name.[37] Miss Bergbom explained to us that when Pseudolus asks Charinus whether there's anything to Simmia, and Charinus answers "plenty of the stinking goat," that was a pun on *Quid sapit?*, which could be understood as meaning either "is he sharp?" or "does he smell?," and *hircus*, the goat, was a Roman term for stinky armpits. Pseudolus then jokes that Simmia needs to wear "a tunic with long sleeves" to cover up the sweaty underarms—and Miss Bergbom explained that wearing long sleeves was considered effeminate. Any surprise, then, that they gave the role of Simmia to Maiju, who could not only do both effeminate and macho but give audiences the idea that underneath the costumes and the make-up the actor playing both roles was in fact female?

I would have loved to play Simmia myself, of course, but Maiju was not only far more experienced and better established in the Finnish Theater: ta was a far better actor than I ever was.

Which role did they give me? The whore with the grammatically neutered name, Phœnicium. A non-speaking role. I was onstage for less than a minute.

Did I want more? Did I chafe at the peripheral parts I was typically given? I'm not sure, to tell you the truth. I suppose I'm not the most self-aware creature to walk the earth. (Am I a creature at all? Or just a two-dimensional drawing cut out of paper?)

I was new, I told myself. I was glad to be cast at all.

And I did love that neutered name.

---

[37] I believe the character's name in Plautus is actually Simmias—a man's name. But perhaps the -s was missing from Emilie Bergbom's imaginary translation? [Tr.]

Benjamin Leino, who was maybe fifty at the time, and married to Mimmy Hellstein—both had been fixtures in the Finnish Theater since it opened back in the early seventies, and for fifteen years Mr. Leino had been famous for his recurring interpretation of King Lear—was to play Simo, Calidorus's father and the slave Pseudolus's master; but he was made up to impersonate Mr. Bergbom. In the dress rehearsal the likeness was uncanny: the slicked-back hair; the bushy eyebrows over the prominent brow ridge; the intense and maybe a touch aggressive but intelligent cast to the eyes; the jutting chin accentuated by a perfectly constructed version of Mr. Bergbom's white bristly Vandyke beard. Mr. Leino had mastered the master's walk and voice, too. We all had to bite our tongues to stifle titters.

Edvard Himberg, an old-timey character actor and opera singer who had also been working in the theater since it opened, despite the fact that he was a fat drunk,[38] was given the role of Pseudolus, because he looked exactly like him—well, with his thinning hair dyed ginger: "A certain red-haired fellow, pot-bellied, with thick calves, swarthy, with a big head, sharp eyes, red face, and very large feet," as he's described in the play. Miss Bergbom told us that the ancients claimed this was Plautus's comic self-portrait.

So the plot is that Simmia, played by my Maiju, is the newly arrived slave who is brilliant at disguise, and is recruited by Pseudolus to impersonate Harpax, the envoy of the Macedonian officer who has bought Phœnicium, the whore that Simo's son

---

[38] If Edvard Himberg did play Pseudolus, it was as a ghost: Himberg died of complications from alcoholism in 1885, 16 years before this imagined production, and in fact was forced to retire from the Finnish Theater five years before that, in 1880. Apart from Himberg's posthumous performance and the fact that no play by Plautus has ever been staged in Finland—well, and the fact that Maiju Lassila and J I Vatanen were Algot Untola's heteronyms, not actual Finnish actors—all the rest of this could have happened. [Tr.]

Calidorus is in love with, from Ballio the pimp. The Macedonian officer has paid only 15 of the agreed-upon 20 minæ, and has sent Harpax to pay the remaining 5 minæ and bring Phœnicium back to Macedonia from Athens, where the play is set. Calidorus and Phœnicium, who are madly in love but can't afford to buy her (my!) freedom, are weeping and contemplating suicide, till Pseudolus promises to free Phœnicium that very day. He pretends to be Ballio's butler and steward and tries to get Harpax to give him the 5 minæ; Harpax refuses, but gives him the letter and token sent by the Macedonian officer. Pseudolus borrows the 5 minæ from Charinus and gives the money and letter and token to Simmia, whom he has dressed up as Harpax; Simmia-as-Harpax gives it all to Ballio and retrieves me. When the real Harpax arrives with the money Ballio takes him to be an impostor recruited by Pseudolus, and general merriment ensues.

The Finnish audiences loved the play. It was a huge hit. It was reviewed by Juhani Aho in *Päivälehti*, [39] and he praised all the performances, especially Mr. Himberg's and Maiju's.

But let me close this chapter by telling you the weirdly wonderful thing that occurred backstage during the dress rehearsal. Maiju had changed a line. After equipping Simmia for the deception, Pseudolus says ta's a clever fellow, and Simmia is supposed to say "And so are you too, who are quite my equal with your mischievous tricks and lies"—but Maiju said instead "with your tricky layers of deceptive personalities." In the next

---

[39] *Päivälehti* is literally "Day Paper"; it was founded in 1889, and in 1894 became the house organ of the left wing of the Young Finnish Party. Juhani Aho (1861-1921), the important Finnish novelist, was one of the founders; we've just seen the National Theater people meeting him in Kappeli a few pages before (p. 44). The paper was liberal and strongly oriented toward Finnish independence; it was shut down in 1904 when it alluded very delicately to the assassination of the Russian Governor-General Nikolai Ivanovich Bobrikov (1839-1904). Almost immediately, however, it was recreated as *Helsingin Sanomat* ("The Helsinki News"), today Finland's premier daily paper. [Tr.]

scene, scene 2, Simmia pulls off the deception, convinces Ballio that ta is the true envoy of the Macedonian officer, and is taken into Ballio's house to get Phœnicium; scene 3 is a quick one, Pseudolus biting his nails while waiting to see who emerges from the house; and scene 4 is the one where Maiju brings me out in tears and assures me that ta isn't really taking me to Macedonia, but to Calidorus and love and freedom.

As soon as we exited at the end of scene 4, my only scene and Maiju's last in the play, Mr. Leino, who was standing there in the wings, said sternly in Mr. Bergbom's voice:

"Maiju, you must recite the lines as written. You don't get to rewrite the play to suit your own little imagination."

Maiju, still in character as the rough military man Harpax who had just saved me, stopped, looked up at him, thought for a moment, and said in a gruff impatient Harpaxian voice, "Well, Mr. Simo Bergbom, why don't you just fire both of those shirkers?"

Mr. Leino, pretending to be flustered but still endeavoring to be stern, stammered "W-what shirkers? Both? I—"

Maiju, still in Harpax's gruff tones: "Maiju Lassila and that obscene epicene Simmia."

"W-what?"

"Fire 'em," ta growled as Harpax, "and I'll impersonate 'em in the play."[40]

Over Maiju's shoulder I spotted the real Mr. Bergbom following the exchange with a smiling shake of his head.

---

[40] That kind of impersonation, of course, is also what novelists do with heteronyms and pseudonyms, and with narrators and characters. It's also what pseudotranslators do with source authors.

Except of course that in this case it was the *impersonation*, Harpax— well, no, it was the impersonation of Harpax *by Simmia*, who was being impersonated by Maiju—that was offering to impersonate the actor and ta's character. That would be sort of like J I Vatanen offering to imper-sonate both the imaginary source author (which in a sense ta did, though actually of course it was the other way around) and the pseudotranslator (which is just funny). [Tr.]

12

Some more pictures Maiju took and developed in this period (1902):

A photo of the Finnish National Theater building, a view of it across the cobblestoned Railway Square, with hundreds of people standing and chatting or walking through the square.

A photo of the train station on that same square, taken on the same day just a few minutes later.

A crowd of the theater-going elite in their finest attire, waiting to be let into the Finnish National Theater for a performance. When I asked how ta had managed to take that photo when ta should have been in make-up for the performance, Maiju just smiled.

An upper-class woman walking with her two very small daughters, maybe two and three years old, along Rahapajankatu ("Mint Street") on Katajanokka.

A photo of workers ringed around their horse-drawn truck near some flatbed freight train cars in the train yard along Rahapajankatu, Katajanokka.

A photo of Katajanokka and beyond, taken from the south, from up in the astronomical "star tower" in the University of Helsinki Observatory just across the water. The observatory is perched on a high hill called Star Tower Mountain. I followed Maiju on this photo shoot as well, climbed up to the viewing terrace of the star tower—without touching the ground.

A photo of two uniformed Russian officers and a uniformed

boy on the deck of their ship docked at the Baltic Fleet Marine Barracks.

A photo of the shipyard at the southern tip of Helsinki, looking across South Harbor to Katajanokka.

A photo of Market Square, packed with people, taken from just across the water on the western edge of Katajanokka, with four or five vendors selling things from their boats in the foreground.

A photo of the same Market Square after the vendors and booths have been removed at the end of the working day. Trash everywhere, with stray dogs and pigeons having a field day.

A photo of the Kaivohuone ("Well House"[41]) variety theater, with the covered outdoor stage on the left and neat rows of benches for the audience on the right.

A summer photo of coachmen and their horse-drawn vehicles, for rent, for freight, and for express couriers, crowding the sidewalk by the Esplanade.

A photo of *flaneurs* striding down the center path in the

---

[41] Kaivohuone or "Well House" takes its name from a mineral water bath and well built in the 1830s on the southernmost peninsula of Helsinki; the area around it was developed into a park called Kaivopuisto, or "Well Park." The Finnish elite had been in the habit of traveling to the mineral water baths in Central Europe, but Tsar Nikolai I had banned foreign travel for all Russian aristocrats; in response, baths had been opened in other Finnish cities, but with minimal success, so a more luxurious one was opened in Helsinki, with far greater success. It was so popular, in fact, and so highly regarded—compared favorably with the famous baths in Central Europe—that it became a coveted destination for the upper classes all across Russia. Outdoor theater and musical performances were arranged there, drawing top performing artists from all over Europe; eventually restaurants and other performance venues were opened in the area as well. The bath's popularity waned in the 1850s and dried up entirely in the 1860s.

The Well House or Kaivohuone was the original building that, as its name suggests, housed the well; it still exists in the northern part of Kaivopuisto, and nowadays is a restaurant. [Tr.]

Esplanade in the autumn, the men in tall shiny cylindrical top hats. That French word again. Did it just mean upper-class men? That's what I saw in the photo.

A photo of a skiing party, sixteen men and women, posing with their skis leaning against their shoulders and poles in hand, in Kaivopuisto ("Well Park").

A photo of a beer coachman sitting side-saddle on a huge barrel of beer strapped down on his horse-drawn cart in the yard of the Sinebrychoff brewery;[42] three adults and a child stand about fifty paces back in the snow, with the brewery building behind them. Finland's oldest brewery, making its most popular beer, in a huge park in Hietalahti ("Sand Bay"), near where I used to live in Rööperi.

---

[42] The Russian entrepreneur Nikolai Petrovich Sinebryukov (1789-1848) started his career as a restauranteur on Viapori Island, but in 1819, just ten years after Finland became a Grand Duchy of Russia, he obtained permission to buy a seven-hectare lot in Helsinki; on it he built his brewery, but most of that land he planted as a park. The brewing company was bought out by Carlsberg in 1999, but Koff—or, as Finns say it, Koffi—is still an extremely popular beer in Finland. [Tr.]

13

An interesting thing happened in early June, 1904, in the Mäntymäki Zoo.[43] I heard there was going to be an event there, and walked over. It turned out to be a Workers' Party gathering called to protest what the speakers called our "unnatural" voting rights situation; but there were also speeches about Prohibition, which the Workers' Party supported and wanted to see voted into law, and the eight-hour working day. The interesting part happened next: a group of men wearing hoods stormed the speakers' platform, and one of them stepped to the front and began shouting to the crowd: "Stop the tyrannical violence, down with Plehve, Bobrikov, and our spineless Senate! Long live freedom!"

The crowd sucked in a hoarse collective breath, then cheered. The police rushed the stage, but the men in hoods had disappeared—removed their hoods and blended with the crowd, no doubt. Arrests were made, but they never found the rabble-rouser.

---

[43] The "Zoo" in Mäntymäki, at the north end of Töölö Bay, has never been a zoo; it's just a park. It started being called Eläintarha, or "Zoo," in the 1870s, on the model of the Djurgården in Stockholm—djurgården in Swedish is literally "animal garden," and while nowadays it does mean "zoo," the park in Stockholm was originally, in the sixteenth century, an "animal garden" reserved as the king's hunting ground. In the early 1880s a plan did arise to create a zoo in Mäntymäki, but the zoo was opened in 1889 on Korkeasaari ("High Island") instead. [Tr.]

But I knew who it was. I would recognize that voice anywhere. It was M.

A week later, Bobrikov was assassinated. A man named Eugen Schauman shot him, then shot himself.

All over the country, Finns celebrated. We heard later that Finns abroad celebrated even more riotously. In Finland, we had to be slightly more circumspect.

The Russian papers reported that Finns were shocked by the murder, because Bobrikov was universally beloved in Finland. *Da ush*, as the Russians say.[44]

Eugen Schauman's father was a general, a Senator, and a Privy Councilor, a man named Fredrik Waldemar Schauman. He was arrested and taken to St. Petersburg, locked up in Peter and Paul Fortress, where he was questioned for several months, before more lenient winds began to blow and he was freed.

The new Governor-General, Prince Ivan Obolensky, picked up where Bobrikov left off, implementing the mandated Russification measures, but more slowly and more mildly, and with total transparency. Finns relaxed a little.

But then in July two more big events happened. In early July the Japanese successfully attacked the Russian Pacific Fleet's base in Port Arthur, China,[45] and Russia was at war

---

[44] That's the pronunciation of Да уж (*da uzh*), which means something like "yeah right." [Tr.]

[45] Port Arthur was the British colonial name for what in Chinese is Lüshunkou. Because it was/is a warm-water port located at the strategic southern tip of Liaodong Peninsula, where it controlled access to northern Yellow Sea routes and Tianjin, the Japanese seized it in the Sino-Japanese war of 1894-1895, but had to cede it when France, Germany, and Russia attacked immediately after the end of that war. In 1897 Russia managed to force China to cede a lease of the Liaodong Peninsula and railway right-of-way from Port Arthur and Dalian to Harbin on the Russian border, thinking that this would promote Russian economic influence through access to shipping routes and so enhance its security. Japan seethed at all this: they believed the peninsula rightly belonged to them. Hence the attack in 1904 and the Russo-Japanese war. [Tr.]

with the Japanese; and in late July von Plehve was assassinated (and Algot Untola fled back to Finland).

In October 1905 Russia lost the war to Japan, and Russian workers declared a general strike. That strike spread quickly to Finland as well. In Russia it led to a revolution; in Finland it completely shut down the Russification project—for a while. The Constitutional Party demanded the removal from office of Russian citizens illegally appointed to Finnish leadership positions, the resignation of collaborationist Senators, and the reconvening of the Finnish Diet; but the larger goal was to create a Parliament based on universal suffrage. I was in the crowd when the Senators officially announced their resignation from the second-floor balcony of the Governor-General's palace. The jubilation in the crowd was mighty.

During the strike Red Guards were formed around the country. The Red Declaration that was read from the balcony of the Tampere City Hall in November, 1905, though, was not politically "red": it was just printed on red paper. It called for universal suffrage, freedom of assembly and association, and an end to censorship. It also called for the resignation of all Senators. It was drafted by the editor of the *People's Paper*, a Social Democratic newspaper, and contained workers' demands; but the Constitutional Party endorsed it as well.

And only a few days later, in a Manifest issued on November 4 in Peterhof, the Tsar caved. All Russification measures were overturned. Constitutional legality was restored. In February of 1906 a new Parliament was created, with universal suffrage—including women and the lower social classes.

We had won!

So we thought.

14

In retrospect, that was the end not of the "years of oppression," as we called them, but of the first phase of oppression. The second phase began in 1908, when Pyotr Stolypin became Prime Minister of Russia and started it all up again: Finland was to be ruled from Russia, and Russian citizens were to have the same rights in Finland as Finnish citizens, especially the right to be appointed to high leadership positions.

The big change in Finland's response to the second phase of Russification was that passive resistance was no longer seen as a realistic course. Finns, including the Kagal, to which M still belonged—I saw him, felt him, fleetingly, in snippets, again and again—began to gear up for armed revolution.

In 1909 Irmari Rantamala's massive Faustian novels, *Harhama* and *Martva*, were published. Rantamala's publisher at Kansa, Kyösti Wilkuna, who would later reject the "Fetching Water" novel I wrote under the Liisa Vatanen pseudonym, announced in print that he had no idea who the "true author" was behind the Irmari Rantamala "pseudonym," which of course started a journalistic feeding frenzy, reviewers guessing at that "true identity." One reviewer even guessed that it was our famous actor colleague at the National Theater, Ida Aalberg!

The fact that Maiju had known Rantamala since their childhood in Tohmajärvi, and indeed since Irmari and M had been best friends throughout their teens and early twenties, made this whole journalistic tempest in a teapot an amusing and therefore welcome distraction from the escalating bad news on the Russification front. Maiju regaled me with stories—like the time Irmari, who frequented the makeshift brothel the Lassila family's laundress Liisa kept in her squalid shack, took M along for an hour of fun, and M was shy, nervous, and hid behind Irmari's back—until the whores refused to sleep with the two and they departed, Irmari disappointed, M relieved.[46]

I was puzzled. *Why would M even go along on an outing like that?* I wondered. *Surely that whole scene would have been distasteful for ta?*

Of course it was, Maiju smiled. *But M wasn't always the assertive and confident behind-the-scenes manipulator ta's become. Ta quite often went along with Irmari's wild ideas, back then.*

Huh.

The whole novel was supposedly 9000 pages long. Parts one and two, each published in three 1000-page volumes, came to 6000; the manuscript of part three, another 3000 pages long, was reportedly lost. Maiju bought volume one of part one and started reading it—frequently clucking and shaking ta's head over it. It was extreme, overblown; it was apparently Symbolist decadence, but it seemed Rantamala wasn't quite up to the challenge of writing a 9000-page decadent novel. Probably nobody would be. Who could sustain that kind of edgy intensity over so many pages?

---

[46] The pseudonymous author of this novel borrows this story from the unfinished and unpublished novel manuscript "Ville Sorsan romaani" ("Ville Sorsa's Novel"). Whoever that author was has apparently forgotten that in *The Last Days of Maiju Lassila* Irmari Rantamala is asexual in the same unspecified way as M, Maiju, and J I. Irmari doesn't play a central role in this novel, but it's clear by the end that ta would have been no more inclined to sleep with a prostitute than M or J I was. [Tr.]

One day Maiju brought home the latest issue of *Suoma-lainen Kansa* ("The Finnish People"[47]), which contained the first part of what would become Eino Leino's long two-part review of *Harhama*, and read it out loud to me. Leino hated the novel, despised it, satirized it mercilessly—and, I had to admit, despite my loyalties to the Tohmajärvi group and the political left, quite enjoyably. Mystifyingly, he identified the novel's style as neo-Romantic; what? We had thought Leino himself was neo-Romantic! He hammered Rantamala for paying the Kansa publishing house to print the novel: "If up until that point Rantamala had been a figure of legend, now, in this writer's eyes at least, based on these lines, he loomed ever larger, becoming a mythical hero, a kind of deity, whose shoelaces no other literary Areopagist than possibly the executive board at the National Bank was fit to untie." "Figure of legend" because not a real person, was the idea. Irmari Ranta-mala must be a pseudonym, and therefore a legendary or mythical creature. "What if," Leino continued, "what if this whole thing," meaning *Harhama* and its mythical author, "what if all of it was actually pure humbug? What if it was all just a gigantic literary Humbert scheme,[48] compared with

---

[47] A periodical published by the right wing of the Young Finnish Party from 1907 to 1911. It was founded as a counterbalance to the party's left-wing paper, which became Finland's major daily newspaper, *Helsingin Sanomat* ("The Helsinki News"). [Tr.]

[48] In her 2013 doctoral dissertation on Algot Untola's heteronyms, Kaisa Kurikka suggests that Leino here may be referring to David Pierre Giottino Humbert de Superville (1770-1849). That Dutch artist and art scholar, draughtsman, lithographer, etcher, and portrait painter, who is generally known by his birth surname Humbert, sought in his three-*volume Essai sur les signes inconditionnels dans l'art* (1827 and 1832) to compile a universal grammar of artistic forms and color theory. He scoured the globe for artifacts that supported his universal grammar; when he realized he would not be able to bring home the massive statues on Easter Island, he made small replicas of them to store in the cabinet where he kept his collection. In his equally satirical review of *Martva*, in fact, Leino calls that novel a "Humbert cabinet."

which all the former and now quite familiar signs of the times would be scarcely discernible to the naked eye? An author who debuts with a 6000-page novel! An author who demands nothing of his publisher and everything of his reader!"

A few weeks later another humorous review appeared in the satirical paper *Tuulispää* ("Squall") under the Nuutti Vuoritsalo byline. Maiju and I always enjoyed his columns, and ta read that one out loud to me as well. The author's real name was Knut Felix Vuoritsalo, but he often wrote under other names as well, such as Felix Hornborg (which was actually his Swedish birth name) and Saint-Boeuf. Instead of ridiculing the novel as too long and written in tasteless Finnish with a tasteless title under a tasteless pseudonym, as Leino had done, Vuoritsalo made a game of it. He claimed he knew A Rantamala personally, indeed that A Rantamala was a "disciple" of his, and based on that supposed acquaintance launched a laugh-out-loud-funny parody of Irmari Rantamala's novel, complete with a sketched portrait of the author, with flames coming out of ta's mouth, an owl on ta's left shoulder, a serpent dangling out of ta's right eye, and a guenon monkey holding a diamond flower perched on top of ta's crowned head. According to Vuoritsalo's clever fantasy, the novel's true author could not be seen because ta was hiding in the brimstone fumes belching out of the work: the true author, he surmised, was actually Old Scratch. In Leino's review ta was a god, in Vuoritsalo's the devil.

Maiju and I shook our smiling heads at the glory of this review. If our novels were ever published, we said, we hoped we might merit something equally absurd.

Leino died in 1926 at the age of 47, and so probably never came into contact with the original Finnish manuscript of *The Last Days of Maiju Lassila*; one wonders whether, had he read that (this) novel, he would have dismissed it too as a Humbert-cabinet. [Tr.]

15

For decades, since the mid-seventies, the number-one theatrical star in Finland had been Ida Aalberg. She was born in the late fifties, and had been the leading lady at the Finnish Theater since it opened, practically. Compared with Maiju she seemed to me old-fashioned and mannered, but the audiences loved her. She often took months off at a time to tour and study abroad, and quite often the Bergboms had to beg her to come back.

So in 1894, before I met the twins, Aalberg received a proposal missive from a German-Russian baron named Aleksander Uexküll-Gyllenband. He had seen her on stage and been smitten with her, and so, without actually having met her, proposed marriage. He had no Finnish at all, spoke German natively and Russian fluently; the letter was in German, which Aalberg could speak and read well enough. Baron Uexküll-Gyllenband was a noted philosopher and advisor to top Russian statesmen; the new string in his bow was this interest in theater, in the Stanislavsky/Moscow Art Theater mode. He was thirty, a few years younger than Aalberg, and had never been married. His dream was to found his own professional theater. That didn't happen until 1919—in Helsinki. The Ida Aalberg Theater. It didn't last long. But I'll return to it. I was involved with it.

Anyway, Aalberg met the baron and soon they were betrothed. They were married in 1895 and settled in St. Petersburg, but the baron also owned a mansion in Helsinki on

Vironkatu and a villa on the Gulf of Finland coast near Viipuri. Baroness Aalberg-Uexküll continued to tour, and took roles at the Finnish Theater as well; in the piece performed on opening day at the newly built Finnish National Theater building she played Aleksis Kivi's Lea.[49]

The point I want to make in telling this story, though, comes a decade later, when Baroness Aalberg-Uexküll signed a contract with the management of the Finnish National Theater to star in four plays in the 1910-1911 season—and things started to go sour. The Bergboms had died in 1905 and 1906, and the new director of the theater, Adolf Lindfors, didn't get along with the baroness, whom he considered a privileged and unreliable diva. One role that had been promised her he gave to another actress; rehearsals for another play he was directing and she was playing the lead in went badly, and the play tanked. Tempers flared; actors and directors and playwrights began to take sides. Maiju and I stayed out of it, but we both suffered inwardly, and privately. Aalberg waxed ardent and eloquent on what the director of the theater should be doing differently, but when asked pointedly whether she would like

---

[49] *Lea* (written 1868) was the only Kivi play performed on stage (1869) before the playwright died at the age of 38 on New Year's Eve, 1872. It was the first play ever performed in Finnish, and as such is celebrated as the fountain of all future Finnish-language drama; hence the decision to perform it at the opening of the Finnish National Theater in 1902.

It's a five-act play based on the story of Zaccheus in the city of Jericho as told in Luke's Gospel; in it Zaccheus's daughter Lea wants to marry her beloved Aram, but Zaccheus wants to marry her to the richer Pharisee Joas. When Lea hears Jesus speak, she is moved to submit to her father's will; Zaccheus is himself in turn moved by this, and wants to meet Jesus as well; as a result, he too converts, as does Aram. In the end he allows Lea to marry her beloved, and Joas rages and curses them all. Kivi portrays Joas as the stereotyped Pharisee: a greedy opportunist.

My translations of four of Kivi's works—his classics, the novel and three plays—were labors of love. I have never been tempted to translate pious *Lea*. [Tr.]

to be the director herself she clammed up. A lot of us believed that taking over the directorship was her true goal; but she and her baron husband were also beginning to plan this new theater that they would be founding instead. It turned out differently—as I say, it didn't get founded until after Ida's death, and didn't last long.

In the spring of 1911 Aalberg was suddenly fired. Everybody who had taken her side in the theater war panicked: what if they were next? Rumors flew. One we heard was that as a young man Lindfors had written impassioned fan letters to Aalberg, but she had not responded; Lindfors was now in a position to exact his revenge. The tour of the provinces that she set out on in the fall of 1911, with my old student friend and mentor Mia Backman in the company, proved to be her last great artistic triumph. She and the baron moved back to St. Petersburg, where she died in 1915, just shy of sixty.

In any case, the upshot of all this was that, sick of the bickering, Maiju quit the theater too. I stayed on; Maiju stayed home to write. Ta's first novel of the year before, *Borrowing Matches*, had been a huge hit—with, as I say, my sort-of namesake as one of the hapless main characters. Part of Maiju's dissatisfaction with the National Theater was that Lindfors had sneered at the four-act comedy ta'd written next, *Kun lesket lempivät* ("Widows in Love"), declaring it "inappropriate" for a prestigious house like the National. Maiju, he'd said, should offer it to the Kaivohuone variety theater, he said, or one that catered more to the "masses." At home that next year Maiju churned out book after book—not just the seven novels and three plays ta published in 1912 but several other book-length things that remained unpublished at ta's passing. None was a bestseller like *Borrowing Matches*, but they all did middling well, and the royalties came to substantially more than Maiju had been making at the National—not that any Lassila was ever hurting for money.

All that writing didn't leave much time for walks or talks with me, of course. So I kept plugging away at my novel—you remember, "The Helpless Ones"—and finally finished it during that year of Maiju's incredible output, and published it in 1913. To, as you'll recall me mentioning, some not insignificant critical acclaim.

Also, though, here's an interesting detail: one day, frustrated with the tangled progress I was making on my novel, I looked over across the table where Maiju and I were both working, looked ta up and down—then slithered down the side of my chair and crawled under the table. Flipping over onto my back, I scooted up to ta's feet, slipped ta's socks off, and lifted both bare feet onto my stomach—under my shirt. Maiju bent over to look down at me and met my gaze, ta's eyebrows lifted in question. I just held that gaze, unblinking. Ta nodded, smiled a little, thought *okay*, and went back to work. I reached both hands up to ta's left knee, laced my fingers over it, and felt the power surging into and through me.

I felt alive. I felt like a real person. My skin rustled like a grate-trapped scrap of paper in a gale. But somewhere in the sewer below the grate, life surged.

I don't know how long I stayed like that. An hour or two, maybe.

16

The outbreak of World War I in the summer of 1914 diluted the Russification measures to the point where in practicality they had no teeth; but it also brought cold and hunger to Finland. During the winters, beginning in 1914-1915, there was precious little fuel for our stoves and water heaters, coal or wood; we lived much of the time indoors with our outdoor winter clothes on, hunkered down against the cold. When we went out, we stood for hours in lines to buy firewood. Sometimes we went two or even three weeks without bathing. In the spring of 1916 the stores ran out of matches. Even if we managed to scrounge up some firewood, we couldn't light it. Electricity was being generated with wood, too, and the stores ran out of candles, so some mornings and evenings we lived in the dark. The water coming out of the faucets was brown and smelled bad. People joked that the brown water was our war-time coffee.

Food production and distribution was disrupted all over Europe. By October 1914 we could no longer buy Baltic herring out of the vendors' boats at Market Square. The Finnish fishermen couldn't fish, the vendors couldn't vend. Eventually fish started being brought in on trains, which seemed absurd to us: fish come from the sea! But fish had to be imported from Russia. Prices skyrocketed. Fortunately, Maiju and I could afford the higher prices, but soon the stores were running out of butter, milk, cheese, meat, coffee, and sugar. By late 1915 Maiju and I were standing in long lines for those staples too every day, as well as for bread, potatoes, and onions. We'd stand in place for hours in frigid temperatures, minus twenty Celsius, jumping up and down in a desperate attempt to stay warm. Sometimes people waiting in line would pass out, collapse to the sidewalk. When one woman got in line wrapped in the blanket from her bed, the people around her joked that she should have brought the whole bed. I think we all agreed that a line of beds would be nice. To pass the time in line we would all bitch about the people we blamed for the shortages: the producers, the distributers, the state, the city, the black market, the rich.

We weren't the rich. We were living off Maiju's royalties and my salary from the theater. But we did have connections. Sometimes M would bring us a bag of food that ta had bought for us on the gray market. We didn't ask questions.

When we got to the counter the battle would begin, all of us fighting to get enough and bitterly accusing others of taking too much. Rationing didn't start until just before the Civil War. Sometimes we would get close to the counter after hours of standing in line, only to be told that they were out of whatever it was we'd been waiting for. Tough luck. Since I was still working at the theater then, and had to be at work after lunch, I would stand in line for two to three hours nearly every morning and Maiju would take the afternoon shift. The two of us would fix breakfast and lunch together, and I would take something along to the theater to eat for dinner.

In the spring of 1916 the so-called "butter war" began. It was fought out in the papers at first, between the left, which wanted the government to control the production and distribution of dairy products, and the right, which wanted to trust private enterprise. In August of 1917 rioters escalated the war into a search-and-seizure operation—more on that in a moment. The Civil War was, in effect, a further escalation of the butter war from those riots to a shooting war.

In March 1917 the February Revolution in Petrograd

spilled over into Helsinki as well—especially, at first, Katajanokka. The Viapori fortress was besieged, just across the ice
from Katajanokka; the Russian military command in Finland
was the Baltic Fleet Marine Barracks where the twins' father
worked. Sailors on the Russian ships docked and anchored
there rose up against their officers, demanding that they raise
the colors of the revolution; on the ships where the officers
were most hated, they were killed. The Russian Vice Admiral
in the Marine Barracks tried to negotiate with the sailors, tried
to convince them that the officers supported the revolution.
The sailors hooted. A day or two later the Vice Admiral too was
killed. Katajanokka was locked down. For two days we
couldn't cross the bridge to line up for food on Market Square.
But in fact the whole city shut down. Nobody went to work.
The sailors from the Russian ships walked across the ice to the
city center and struck up the *Marseillaise*. A few shots were
fired at soldiers from open windows, but for the most part it
was a giant celebration. Tsarist Russia was going down!

Well, it wasn't, yet. But for most of that year we lived in
what felt like a three-ring circus. Every day, it seemed, there
was some new upheaval. It was a time of endless possibility—
so it seemed to us. Anything can happen now! We're free to
do whatever we want—and who knows *what* we'll end up
wanting! All that summer the city streets and especially Senate Square were filled with demonstrations, impassioned ha-
rangues, debates, street theater—all manner of events. There
were parades. There were brass ensembles playing marches.
There was a collective funeral for all those who had lost their
lives in the March Revolution.

Between food lines and my job at the theater, I didn't have
much time to enjoy the festivities; but Maiju did. Once ta had
developed the photos ta had taken on Senate Square, ta would
tell me all about what ta had seen and felt and heard from the
others around ta.

Various unions and other worker groups went on strike,

beginning in the spring and continuing on into the autumn. They had various demands, the prime one being an eight-hour workday. When in mid-August the city council met in the Stock Exchange Building to discuss that particular demand, a mob of thousands gathered outside in that narrow street the building overlooked, shouting slogans and demanding passage of the bill. I managed to join that mob. I was never in the thick of the fray, of course: as was my wont, I stood back and observed. I noticed the presence of Russian soldiers in the mob—hundreds of them, maybe more than a thousand. The crowd was abuzz with what they would do if the city council didn't pass the eight-hour workday bill; the consensus was that they would storm the building. One of the loudest voices in that group arguing *against* violent action was familiar: Algot Untola. Another was Kustaa Rovio, whose voice I didn't recognize but whose face was familiar from the papers: in the spring he had been named Assistant Chief of Helsinki Police, and, when the Chief of Police resigned in protest, Rovio became acting Chief. He was a Social Democrat, but later joined the Finnish Communist Party, and became some kind of top official in Soviet Karelia. He was a Finn who was born in St. Petersburg and spoke both Finnish and Russian fluently. He served as interpreter and negotiator on several delegations from Finland to Petrograd. I read later that it was in his apartment that Lenin hid out during those months between the February and October Revolutions. Anyway, Rovio brought in volunteers armed with batons to control the mob outside the Stock Exchange; it turned out they had been recruited by the right-wingers and came in on horseback wearing white armbands and broke up the mob. That was the beginning of the Civil Guard that eventually turned into the White Army. Nice irony there.

A day or two later, M's and Algot Untola's Tohmajärvi friend Irmari Rantamala, writing in *The Workingman*, condemned the "disorderly" mob outside the Stock Exchange and supported Rovio's action in bringing in white-armbanded volunteers to restore order.

The food shortages got worse. The city finally stepped in and imposed rationing, but even that move couldn't keep up with the worsening situation. More and more people were unemployed and homeless. In the autumn rioting began. People were sick of what seemed like the municipal authorities' total indifference to their suffering. Rumors started circulating about Valio, the powerful conglomerate of seventeen dairies, stockpiling huge quantities of butter and refusing to sell it. The rioters I mentioned a few paragraphs ago broke into dairy warehouses, and to everyone's surprise, there *were* huge stockpiles of unsold butter. The municipal government confiscated those stores and rationed them out. The general sentiment was that all food supplies should be confiscated by the government and rationed out—that private grocers were artificially maintaining shortages to raise prices and gouge the poor to enhance profits. This time when rioters broke into storehouses, however, they found nothing.

That entire autumn was a time of strikes and riots. As one would end, another would begin. Sometimes they would overlap. Many of the groups participating in these actions came armed; sometimes skirmishes ended in violence; sometimes the violence ended in death. The general strike in November,[50]

---

[50] The food, energy, and health-care industries were excluded from the strike. On the first day security men circulated about town, making sure businesses were closed. All seemed orderly, except that the security men were armed—by the Russians, who were hoping the strike would tip Finland into their revolution. On the second day the Russian-armed security men took control of Helsinki—the whole city—and forced the banks and most stubborn businesses to join the strike. Revolution and civil war seemed imminent. The papers were on strike, so no one knew anything. In the next few days the homes of prominent leaders were searched and arrests were made. The strike only lasted a few days, however, as the majority moderates in Parliament refused to yield to the Workers' Guards' demands. Outside Helsinki, however, the general strike led to chaos and violent skirmishes; a total of about two dozen people were killed. [Tr.]

which spread from the October Revolution in Petrograd and broke the ailing Finnish economy, was really just the culmination of a seven-month political carnival.

Not only that: it was also a portal into civil war.

17

Photos taken and developed by Maiju in this period (1914-1917):

A photo of telegram boys lined up before the Telegraph in 1914, ready to run telegrams from the war.

A photo of Market Square from the third (top) floor of the building across the road from its southeast corner, with a tram turning in the foreground and the Stone of the Empress monument in the background right, taken in April, 1916. The Tsar and his wife the Empress had visited Helsinki back in the early nineteenth century, and the monument had been erected in honor of that visit. In the photo in 1916 it was still capped with the bronze globe and imperial Russia's double-headed eagle, which were knocked down by Russian sailors in the February 1917 Revolution.[51]

A photo of the Russian MPs at the bridge to Katajanokka,

---

[51] The tsar was Nikolai I (1796-1855); his wife was Empress Aleksandra Fyodorovna (1798-1860). She was originally Princess Friederike Luise Charlotte Wilhelmine of Prussia, daughter of King Friedrich Wilhelm III (1770-1840, reigned 1796-1840), the king who infuriated Friedrich Schleiermacher during Napoleon's occupation of Prussia, just before his 1813 Academy address "On the Different Methods of Translating." The visit to Helsinki was her first; the red obelisk monument was erected in 1835. The bronze globe and double eagle were broken when the Russian sailors knocked it off by throwing stones at it, but it was saved and restored and reattached to the top of the monument in 1971, the year I arrived in Helsinki as a sixteen-year-old exchange student. The reattaching of that bronze cap was not tied in any way to my arrival. [Tr.]

preventing ingress or egress, in March 1917.

A photo of a cart entrance at Yrjönkatu ("George Street") 25 with a sign saying "New Forest Office," spring 1917. It was actually the secret headquarters of the Active Committee, which was recruiting young Finnish men for the Jäger Movement,[52] to be sent to Germany for military training, but also forging passports for those recruits, smuggling weapons from Germany, and generally preparing for armed revolution.

A photo of the writer Arvid Järnefelt giving one of his infamous lectures to a packed Kallio Church in May 1917.[53]

---

[52] A *Jäger* in German is a hunter, but in Germany the Jägers were a specially trained elite group of light infantrymen. When Hessian Jägers fought in the British Army's attempt to suppress the American Revolution at the end of the 18th century, they adopted the name "Rangers," from Gorham's Rangers (1744-1762) and Roger's Rangers (1755-1761), because they were highly mobile forces, able to "range" across territory quickly. In Finland the Jäger Movement (*jääkäriliike*) began in 1914 among young educated Finnish men who set up secret recruitment centers all over the country; the recruits left Finland surreptitiously through Sweden and proceeded down to Germany for training. At first they fought alongside Germans in the battles for control of Russia's western provinces and dependencies, especially the Baltics and Poland; when the Finnish Civil War broke out, most of them returned to Finland to join the Whites as officers. They were a decisive factor in the Whites' victorious battles even before German troops arrived in April 1918.

The "New Forest Office" advertised lumber in the papers, but when customers showed up looking to buy lumber they were turned away with some excuse. [Tr.]

[53] Järnefelt (1861-1932) gave three of these "church talks," interrupting Sunday services by climbing up into the pulpit and beginning to speak. The anarchist Jean Boldt (1865-1920) participated as well, and what Järnefelt was preaching was basically an extreme form of Tolstoyan pacifism that effectively came to anarchism. As a convert to Tolstoyism he had given up his law career and become a farmer. Because there were some scuffles during his talks, he and Boldt were arrested on violence charges; when the three church talks were published in 1918, he was arrested again and convicted of inciting insurrection, and the entire print run was confiscated and burned; Marshal Mannerheim as Regent issued a pardon in 1919.

A photo of an unidentified speaker haranguing the crowd on Senate Square in June 1917.

A photo of a group of amateur actors staging a political melodrama on Senate Square in July 1917. The bad guys are the capitalists who are gouging the workers, who are of course the good guys.

A photo of rioters breaking into the Farmers' Milk Center at the corner of Salomonkatu ("Salomon Street") and Olavinkatu ("Olaf Street") in August 1917.

A photo of a long food line stretching down Unioninkatu ("Union Street") toward the Hansa butter and cheese shop in August 1917, after the butter riots.

Järnefelt is perhaps the likeliest candidate for actual author of this novel. [Tr.]

18

It wasn't until the February Revolution in Russia, in early 1917, that the new Esser rulers in St. Petersburg, or Petrograd, as it was called by then,[54] restored Finland's autonomy to pre-1899 levels. The Bolsheviks seized power in October; in November the Finnish economy was devastated by a general strike; and on December 6 Finland declared independence from Russia. Russia was politically and militarily and economically in such a shambles that the Bolshevik rulers basically said, "Sure, whatever, do what you have to do."

And we thought: could it be that easy?

But of course it couldn't. It wasn't. One month after the Russians agreed to our independence, in late January, the Civil War broke out. Three more months of misery for everybody.

In the second week of January 1918, I woke in the middle of the night to hear a key in the front door. I swung my feet out of bed and into slippers, stuck my head out of my bedroom doorway like Pinocchio[55]—and saw (who else?) M stamping

---

[54] The city, Peter the Great's "window to Europe," was St. Petersburg from its founding in 1703 till 1914, Petrograd from 1914 till 1924 (after Lenin's death), and Leningrad from 1924 till 1991, when it became St. Petersburg again. [Tr.]

[55] Carlo Collodi's 1883 Italian original *Le avventure di Pinocchio* was first translated into Finnish by another Maiju, Maiju Halonen, in 1906, as *Pinocchion seikkailut: kertomus marionetista* ("The Adventures of Pinocchio: A Tale of a Marionette.") [Tr.]

snow off his boots and shucking his snow-dusted hat and greatcoat. He switched the overhead light on: the clock said 4:15. Early, and pitch-black dark—after all, it was the dead of winter—but a welcome sight.

"M," I said.

And then Maiju looked out, saw M, rushed to give ta a hug.

We grabbed blankets and draped them over our shoulders. M had brought firewood; ta went to light a fire in the Dutch oven, and I went to light a fire under the iron stovetop, for coffee. When all was ready, we sat down at the dining table.

"Sorry to wake you," M said. Serious.

Maiju stifled a yawn, waved a hand. "No, no. Talk."

M raised ta's coffee mug. "A war is brewing," ta said.

"War?" Maiju said. "What, the Russians are attacking?"

"No," M said. "The Russians are done with us. A lot of them have already left. They're clearing out the Marine Barracks."[56]

"Is Dad leaving too?"

"Well, yes, but not leaving Finland. He and Mom have headed up to Tohmajärvi. His job here has vanished with the Russians, obviously. He's calling it retirement."

"Good for him," Maiju said. "So who's fighting the war, if the Russians aren't involved?"

"The war isn't officially being fought yet," M said. "So far just an isolated shoot-out in Sipoo yesterday."

"Between—?"

"The Workers' Guard and the Civil Guard."

---

[56] The so-called "Ice March" of Russia's Baltic Fleet out of Helsinki and Tallinn to Kronstad began in early April as word came of the German expeditionary fleet's imminent arrival in the Gulf of Finland. Kronstad is a port city on Kotlin Island 30 km west of Petrograd; back then it housed the main base of the Russian Baltic Fleet. A British submarine flotilla that had been supporting the Russian fleet stayed behind in Helsinki, and was sunk by the Germans on the Harmaja shoals out on the southern periphery of the Helsinki archipelago. A Russian torpedo boat was also sunk on the shore of Kulosaari ("Wildfire Island") in the Helsinki harbor. [Tr.]

"All Finns?"

"Mostly Finns. They're calling themselves Reds and Whites."

"So it's a class war. The rich and the poor. The bourgeoisie and the proletariat."

"Something like that, yes. But also, maybe, monarchists and communists."

"The Reds want to join the Russian Revolution?"

"Some do. Maybe a lot of them do. But there's internal division on both sides."

"So what makes you think an isolated shootout will turn into a war? Maybe they'll be able to negotiate a compromise?"

"Doesn't look that way. They're arming themselves. They're breaking into armories and stealing the weapons. The Reds had an armored train that the Russians had left; the Whites have commandeered it. The Reds have occupied most of the Governor-General's building downtown. It's looking a lot like war."

The three of us sat silent for a while, processing that news. It was hard to imagine—hard to accept the reality of what M was telling us. Finns killing Finns? Brother killing brother?

"So, M," Maiju finally said, slowly. "Tell us. What side are you on?"

M met Maiju's gaze: "Neither."

Maiju snorted. "Come on, M. You're involved. I know you are. You're a behind-the-scenes guy. You're not Switzerland."

"I don't want to endanger you two by telling you much," M said. "Let's just say I'm on Finland's side."

"What does that mean?"

"I'm on the side of a future independent Finland."

"That sounds like youthful idealism."

M laughed. "It does, doesn't it? I'm 45. We're 45. Happy birthday, by the way. Nine days ago. Sorry I couldn't be here."

Maiju shrugged. "Happy birthday to you too. J I was here."

"So I'm not young. I'm idealistic, maybe, but I've earned it.

And what I believe is that if the Reds win, we'll be a Soviet Socialist Republic in the USSR, and if the Whites win, we'll have a puppet government installed and run by the Germans."

"The Germans? Why the Germans?"

"Don't you remember how in October we were all afraid the Germans were going to invade Finland? The sirens went off in the evening and the whole city went dark and nobody knew what that meant? And we all expected Zeppelins to fly over us and drop bombs?"

"Oh. Right."

"And the Americans refused to sell us food, because they were so sure we were about to be overrun and occupied by an enemy force?"

"Huh. I didn't know about that one."

"Anyway, a lot has changed since then, but the Germans' desire to contain Russia by controlling Finland and the Baltics and Poland hasn't. The Swedes are no longer in the game. They're going to sit this one out. So Germany is the entire European opposition to the Soviet Union. They have every possible interest in making sure the Whites win. They've trained two thousand Finnish boys as Jägers. Those troops will return to Finland to fight on the Whites' side, as officers. The Reds are a disorganized bunch without military training. I doubt they'll last long against the Whites—especially if Germany sends their own troops to join the battle. And we think they will."

"The Bolsheviks in Russia won't support the Reds?"

"Doubtful. They're already overextended, trying to consolidate power. Their Civil War will overshadow ours in their efforts, given the massive territory the Bolsheviks will have to control."[57]

---

[57] The Russian White Army did not cave until 1923 in Yakutia—but continued to fight in Central Asia and Khabarovsk Krai until 1934. Finland wasn't the only periphery that managed to break free in those years: Estonia, Latvia, Lithuania, and Poland did as well. [Tr.]

"So now you're going to—?"

"Do everything in my power, our power, to thwart a German takeover of Finland once the Whites do win. Lay the groundwork for a successful transition to actual independence. Finnish sovereignty."

Maiju and I sat digesting this proclamation now for a minute or two. How would one go about doing any of that? Talking to people? Aiding both sides? Thwarting both sides? Judicious assassinations?

"What should we be doing?" Maiju asked.

"Staying safe," M replied.

"How? Not going out? How do we buy food?"

"I'll try to keep you supplied whenever I can. Once or twice a week, probably. Maybe more. But yes, you'll need to go out. Just do it carefully. Be sensible. There's going to be shooting in the streets, most likely."

"In Helsinki?"

"All over southern Finland. And yes, in Helsinki too. Helsinki will most likely be controlled by the Reds, which means apart from me you'll only have access to Red-tinted news. Algot and my old friend Irmari are writing for *The Workingman*; they'll be feeding the whole city Red propaganda. White propaganda won't be much worse, probably. But there will be skirmishes in the city. Even possibly on Katajanokka. If you hear gunfire or see people running by outside the windows, don't go out."

"Hoo," Maiju breathed. "Our life is going to change."

"With luck," M said, "the big change will be an exponential increase in boredom. You'll be stuck inside a lot more."

I spoke up for the first time. "Will the theaters stay open? Will I be going to work?"

M smiled. "Time will tell. My guess is, no. They won't stay open. But we'll see."

19

And so our war-time began. As M had predicted, it was boredom punctuated with sharp stabs of anxiety, whenever a rat-a-tat-tat of gunfire seemed especially close by. It was worst at night—not that there was more gunfire then, but that it always seemed to start up just as I was drifting off to sleep. Gunfire, or trucks rumbling by on the cobblestones, or loud and sometimes panicky shouting. Suddenly I was no longer sleepy. I would tell myself I was safe, no one was coming for us in our apartment, force my heart rate back down to sleepable levels, start drifting off again ... and rat-a-tat-tat.

M was as good as ta's word: stopped by two and sometimes three times a week with a burlap sack of groceries and the latest news of the war. But we still had to go out to line up for food on the days ta didn't come. Sometimes, standing there for hours, we would hear gunfire down the street, or around the corner, and our hearts would start beating in our throats. Sometimes we would pass dead bodies in the street. It was sickening the first few times; gradually we became inured to the sight.

The theaters did close. They were requisitioned by the Red Guards as meeting places and—nice irony in this—staging areas for military operations. That meant Maiju and I could stand simultaneously in separate food lines. Oh joy.

One day Maiju was standing in a bread line when a stocky bearded man walking along the line toward its tail stopped and stared at ta, then slowly raised his right hand and waggled his index finger at ta.

"Maiju Lassila," he said. "Right? The former actress and of late prolific novelist. We've met at Kappeli several times. You were with the National Theater bunch."

Then Maiju remembered: Eino Leino, the poet. He was a little younger than the twins, maybe forty.

I squinted at him a little. *Is he drunk?*

Probably, Maiju replied. *But he holds it well.*

A little unsteady on his feet.

Aren't we all.

"Yes, hello, nice to see you, Mr. Leino," Maiju said.

"What do you think of all this, then, Miss Lassila? Some kind of Nordic insanity, wouldn't you say?"

"What, the war?" Maiju said carefully. And, at Leino's nod: "I suppose."

I snorted. *"Miss"?*

Maiju was dressed like a man and didn't have any obvious female features. *But*, ta laughed, *I've got this female name.*

"You know," the poet said, allowing his voice to swell a little dramatically, "walking over this way along North Esplanade I passed a ragtag gang led by an honest-to-goodness mental patient with a rifle, which he was waving about erratically, his eyes wild, his teeth bared up to the tops of his gums, and the most alarmingly deranged expression jumping around all over his face. And I thought yes, this, this right here is the very picture of their little rebellion! This gang of misshapen Finnish louts led by a madman, and not a gram of honesty or integrity to divvy up amongst them! Helsinki is overrun by riffraff, by scum, by the worst of the country's vermin! But then, can you imagine? Their leader shouted at me: 'No coming! No come! Shooting!' Heavy Russian accent. He wasn't a Finn after all, but a damn Russian Red Communist, and our boys following him like lambs to the slaughter."[58]

I could feel the people around Maiju beginning to stir in irritation. Who was this guy, dressed like a rich man, who hated the poor this much? And who was Maiju, whom he recognized by name?

Apparently Leino was still sober enough to feel it as well, as he rubbed his face thoughtfully, looked up and down the line, and made to walk on.

Before he left, though, he launched one last salvo: "It is my considered opinion, Miss Lassila, that any legitimately vested authority in the world, even the most totalitarian state, is better than rule by riffraff," he said. "But," he sighed, casting his eye down along the line again, "rule by riffraff would appear to be an unavoidable stage in the history of every revolution."

And he lurched into motion again.

Once he was out of earshot, a man standing near Maiju asked who that man was.

"I don't know," ta said. "I've never laid eyes on him in my life."

"But he called you by name," the man protested. "You called him by his."

"That's not my name," Maiju said calmly. "And he called me 'Miss.' You saw it, the man was drunk. He probably didn't even hear that name I made up for him."

---

[58] I should mention that Prof. Julius Nyrkki of the University of Nuorgam took issue (what else would one expect from that pit bull?) with this rather negative portrayal of Eino Leino, whom patriotic Finns consider a national treasure—and blamed *me* for inventing it! But I Googled "Vatanen's" Finnish and found that in fact Leino himself wrote those words in his memoir of the Civil War, *Helsingin valloitus* ("The Conquest of Helsinki," Helsinki: Minerva, 1918), on pages 10-11 and 24. Presumably the pseudonymous Finnish author writing the novel in the late teens or early twenties (or whenever) borrowed that scene straight from the White horse's mouth. [Tr.]

"Oh." And several of the people around nodded, as if satisfied.

Maiju and I knew what they were really thinking, though, because we were thinking the same: *Well, that passed the time nicely.*

20

The Germans arrived in April. Suddenly the two and a half
months we'd had of incidental shooting in the streets seemed
like a walk in the park. Over the course of two days in mid-
April the Germans occupied Helsinki, stamping out the last
vestiges of Red resistance. That meant fighting in the streets.
Not in Katajanokka, thank God; but we later heard of people
spending the entire day lying on their floors as the bullets flew,
smashing their windows. Some people on higher floors,
feeling less vulnerable to the firefights below, threw parties,
eating and drinking with friends while watching the show out
their windows. Less timorous rubberneckers, including scores
of children, went out into the streets to watch the action.

Maiju went out too, with ta's camera. My friend and flat-
mate the war photographer.

I stayed in. No one would ever mistake me for "less timorous."

The shooting was over on the 13th. Early in the morning of
the 14th I again woke to the sound of a key turning in the lock
on the front door.

It was M, of course. The news was grim.

"I'm here to move you two to a safehouse," ta said without
preamble.

"Move us?" Maiju protested. "Why?"

"They've arrested Algot Untola as a Red agitator. You're in
danger."

"What could Algot's arrest possibly have to do with us?"

"Not both of you," M said. "You, Maiju."

"Why me?"

"Because Algot published a book back in 1912 under your name."

"B-but ..."

"I know, it seems far-fetched. But hear me out. Yesterday when they grabbed him, he was the last man left in the editorial offices of *The Workingman*. He had sent Irmari away, and for the previous few days he had been putting out the paper single-handed. Pretty vicious Red propaganda. Slaughter all the Whites, men, women, and children. That sort of thing."

"And?"

"And he kept publishing those stories under Irmari's name. A pseudonym that wasn't Maiju Lassila, obviously—but once the White leaders discovered that all those stories were being written by one man, they started looking into pseudonyms he'd used before, and found that novel he published under your name in 1912."

"Oh. Jesus."

"Yeah. So it's only a matter of time before they come looking for you, and arrest you too."

"Thinking that I'm somehow in on the Red propaganda thing as well."

"Exactly." M paused for a moment. "And when I say 'only a matter of time,' I don't mean weeks. I mean days. Possibly even hours."

"Wow."

"That's what I said. Listen, do you have any way to disguise yourself?"

"Both of us, right?" I asked.

"Yes, both. Best to move you both."

Maiju thought for a moment. "I think we have some theater props here somewhere. A wig, a hat, a cane, that kind of thing."

"Why don't you go round that stuff up. You two disguise

yourselves as best you can. I'll pack up your food. What else do you want to take?"

"My camera," Maiju said.

"Are you sure you're going to be needing that?"

"I'm sure."

"Okay. Take some socks and underwear, but not much in the way of outer clothes. Whenever you go out you'll need to be disguised, preferably in a different guise each time."

"I guess we'll pick up used clothes and accessories at the markets."

"Right."

And so we left. Were evacuated, I suppose you could say. M told us that we were headed for Rööperi, where I used to live. M remembered that, in fact, and as we walked ta asked me what I knew about the district. When I said I didn't know much, ta said that Rööperi had been a poor working-class area for a long time, starting in the eighteenth century: sailors and fishermen living in wooden shacks. But that began to change, ta said, in the 1870s, when Katajanokka was razed and began to be rebuilt; the five-story brownstone the twins and I had been living in for more than twenty years was one of the newer buildings built after the urban renewal project tore down the dilapidated wooden shacks and their denizens had had to move out. Mostly, it turned out, they moved to Rööperi—and a lot of them were criminals and smugglers. That gave Rööperi a bad reputation. I of course started reviewing my memories of my mother's cousin, his mysterious sullenness, what he might have been hiding behind that protective coloring. According to M the district's reputation was good cover for us.

He took us to the upper floor in a small two-story wooden house. We had our own separate entrance off the front porch; the door opened onto a staircase. The people who lived below us had fled the war in January; we should be left in peace. In that upstairs apartment we sat out the rest of the war.

Which wasn't long, in fact. One month. The war was officially declared over on May 15. The Senate, which had been
in exile in Nikolainkaupunki, now restored to its original
name, Vaasa, near where I grew up, had returned to Helsinki
in early May; M told us that upon their return they were
received not by the leadership of the White Army but by a
division of the German Baltic expeditionary force, complete
with a military band playing "Alte Kameraden." P E Svinhufvud was appointed Regent of Finland, but everyone knew that
Major General Rüdiger von der Goltz, commander of the
German forces, was the actual Regent behind the scenes—a
fact that triggered M and that whole group into escalating
their own behind-the-scenes action.[59] Marshal Mannerheim,
the commander of the Finnish White Army, organized a
victory parade through Helsinki on May 16.[60] The struggle for

---

[59] Pehr Evind Svinhufvud (1861-1944) was an aristocrat who won Finns'
support through his adamant advocacy of Finnish legal rights during the
Russification period; his advocacy got him exiled to Siberia for two years,
but he was able to return during the February Revolution. He served as
Head of the Finnish Senate in exile during the Civil War and was appointed
Regent at its end. Given the power imbalance between Finns and Germans,
however, even Svinhufvud as Regent advocated for the coronation of
Friedrich Karl, Prince of Hessen, as Finland's king; the "actual Regent"
Count Rüdiger von der Goltz (1865-1946) supported Prince Oskar, son of
Kaiser Wilhelm I. When Germany lost the war and the monarchy was
overthrown in December, German control ended and Finland became a
republic instead. Svinhufvud stepped down as Regent on December 12,
1918, and Marshal Mannerheim took over as Regent. Svinhufvud served as
President of Finland from 1931 to 1937. [Tr.]

[60] Carl Emil Mannerheim (1867-1951), Marshal of Finland, had served
nearly three decades as an officer in the Russian imperial army before
becoming the commander of the White forces in the Civil War. He had
fought in the Russo-Japanese War in 1904-5 and in Poland, Galicia,
Romania, and Bukovina in the First World War; before that latter war
broke out, he was promoted to General. Mannerheim was made Regent in
December 1918, and served in that capacity until the first president was
elected in the summer of 1919. Mannerheim lost that election to K J Ståhlberg, mainly because the Social Democrats in the government refused to

control of the symbolism.

It only later occurred to me to ask whether M had done the same for Irmari Rantamala as ta had done for us: moved ta to a safe house, urged ta to change ta's name and disguise taself when ta went out. Irmari Rantamala was almost certainly in bigger danger than Maiju. Ta had published pages and pages of angry Red propaganda under ta's own name. Had M spirited ta out of war-torn southern Finland entirely?

---

vote for the former White commander. He later served as commander of the Finnish forces in World War II, and from 1944 to 1946 served as Finland's sixth president. Even today, more than a century after the Civil War, the left still despises Mannerheim—I once heard a university student call him a "rat"—while the right reveres him as one of the greatest Finns who ever lived. [Tr.]

21

Some photos Maiju took and developed during this time (1918):

A photo of the exploded wreck of a Russian torpedo boat on the Kulosaari shore in March.

A photo of a Red Guard unit marching down North Esplanade in early April.

A photo of newly arrived German troops marching down Rautatiekatu ("Railway Street") in mid-April. [61]

A photo of Senate Square in the pouring rain during the Civil War, with mounted German cavalry troops and horse-drawn carts, some carrying six officers, others carrying cannons.

A photo of Finnish kids chatting with a mounted German soldier standing guard during the Civil War.

A photo of German troops storming the Ilmala weather station at the top of its granite hill in mid-April.

A photo of the Turku Barracks on fire. [62]

---

61 The German expeditionary fleet arrived in early April: a division of 10,000 troops came ashore in Hanko on April 3; they were the ones that would take Helsinki from the Reds on April 12-13, and a host of other cities in southern Finland in the next week or two. A brigade of 3000 troops arrived from across the Gulf of Finland in Tallinn, landing in Loviisa, 90 km to the east of Helsinki on the coast, on April 7. [Tr.]

62 Located in the country's southwest corner, Turku (Åbo in Swedish) was Finland's largest and most important city until the early nineteenth century, when Finland was occupied by Russia and made an autonomous

A photo of the Helsinki Workers' House on fire.[63]

Russian Grand Duchy; at first it was the capital of autonomous Finland, but in 1812 Tsar Alexander I moved the capital to Helsinki. The Turku Barracks, however, is in Helsinki. It was built in 1833 to house the Finnish Army, which moved there from what became the Marine Barracks in Katajanokka. It had been occupied by the Reds but was shelled and mostly destroyed by the German troops on April 12. [Tr.]

63 The red lantern hung by the Reds from the Workers' House tower had been the unofficial declaration of war back at the end of January. It had been a major recruiting site for Red Guards in the months since. On April 13, 1918, German troops declared a 90-minute truce to give the Red Guards holed up inside a chance to surrender. When they refused, the Germans shelled it until they did. [Tr.]

THE PIVOT

(May 15 – 21, 1989)

The Civil War ended on May 15, 1918.

Did Maiju and I come out of hiding then? Did we put aside our disguises? Did we move back to Katajanokka?

No.

Both the Whites and the Reds had been employing terror tactics throughout the war: slaughtering not only prisoners of war but civilians. Both sides had been publishing the gory details of the other side's terror in their propaganda sheets from the beginning. But now that the Whites had won, and 76,000 Red soldiers were in prison in the Viapori fortress and other sites around the city, the White Terror was unleashed in full force. It lasted one hundred days—all summer, until late August.

The act of the White Terror that impinged most direly on us was that Algot Untola was sentenced to death as a Red agitator.

On May 21 he was loaded onto a transport ship in chains, along with many other Red prisoners, to be taken to Viapori prison for execution. En route, however, he was pushed overboard and shot to death in the water.

So no, Algot's "pseudonym" Maiju Lassila could not come out of hiding. We could not put aside our disguises. We could not move back to our apartment on Katajanokka. M told us that the police had searched our apartment and canvassed the neighbors, asking about our movements. Senator Oswald Kairamo, who had demanded the arrest and execution of Algot—and been present on the transport ship when Algot was murdered—had been raging at the chief of police, demanding that his operatives find and arrest Maiju Lassila.

For us, in a very real sense, the Civil War continued.

AFTER

(late May, 1918 – mid-February, 1919)

21

In the aftermath of the war, Maiju and I still went out for walks, of course. It was dangerous, if M was to be believed; but we couldn't stand being cooped up inside four walls for weeks and months. Or even days. We had to get out.

And of course, as we'd done during the month before the war ended, we continued to go out in disguise. Some days we went out as two rich industrialists, thinking that would be the kind of person the Whites would respect—in pin-striped double-breasted suits, starched shirts, neckties or bow ties, our hair slicked down close to our skulls and crowned with top hats, walking as if we owned every square centimeter we trod upon. Some days we went out as a middle-aged heterosexual couple madly in love, alternating genders and testing which of us could do each better. I always thought Maiju did both the man and the woman better, but ta disagreed, insisting that I was better at being the woman.

This one day in late May that I want to tell you about, we went out as two stout and relatively elderly working-class women, walking slowly, Maiju bent over a little, me with a hitch in my step. Warm summer had arrived in Helsinki; it was a glorious day to be out for a walk. And somehow being in disguise only enhanced our pleasure at the sun and the light breeze.

As was our custom on these walks, we first looked for street vendors selling old clothes and other items—the war had impoverished many Finns, destroyed homes, killed fathers and brothers and sons, and the only way many had to bring in money for food and rent was by selling off their possessions. We thought of our shopping forays mainly as acquiring costumes and props for our walks; but we also tried to give the sellers a little more than they were asking.

This day we found nothing along the meandering course our legs chose for us, so we headed over to Market Square across the bridge from Katajanokka, poked around there for a bit, found a few useful things, bundled them up, and then cast a longing glance out to the island on which we used to live. We didn't go walking there often, for fear that we would be sought in that district where we had spent a happy twenty-odd years, where Maiju's father used to work—the old Baltic Fleet Marine Barracks stood empty these days, of course, all the Russian ships and officers having gone home—but with the breeze blowing a slight salt tang into our nostrils, the idea of walking around Katajanokka was just too tempting.

We set out along the northern shore, deciding to walk around clockwise, and trudged along in character, slowly, nursing our imaginary aches and pains, picking our laborious way through the train yard between Kanavakatu and Rahapajankatu. The low brick wall along the far edge of the train yard, at the bottom of the hill on which the cathedral stood, was still occupied by the row of old men, still looking like chickens on a fence; as we passed, a few of the men muttered polite greetings to us. Not as if they knew us, but as if they knew women like us, as if their wives and sisters were women just like us, and so deserving of some measure of grudging respect. Again one of them half-stood to ruffle his feathers against the cold, then made to settle himself back down with the others, but stopped mid-settle, as if recognizing us.

"Praskoviya!" he called out. "Agniya!"

Two old-fashioned Russian women's names: who was this

person mistaking us for someone he knew? I kept trudging along; but Maiju recognized the voice and turned.

"Algot?"

"You mean Oiva," the voice cautioned. "Oiva Kairamo, you meant to say."

We turned—and there, sure enough, was something that looked and sounded uncannily like Algot Untola in the flesh. Algot Untola, who had been shot up in the water not far from here, on the way from Santahamina to Viapori: could it be? No. The twins' old friend, back from the dead, with a new name, in case there were vindictive Whites within earshot and they had a mind to kill him again? It couldn't.

But I felt a mighty shudder snake through me.

Maybe it could.

Beside me, I could feel Maiju's reaction as well, spooked, skittish.

"S-so sorry," ta stammered.

I was trembling all over. I could hardly see out of my eyes.

"I mistook you for someone else," Maiju babbled on. "Your voice sounds so much like another friend of mine, who—can't—join us ..."

The Algot-thing brushed itself off, looked both of us enthusiastically in the eye, and said: "How about I join you instead? Huh?"

Maiju took a deep, deep breath. Held it in as long as ta could. Then, heavily:

"Sure, Oiva. Walk with us."

"Let's go," the thing said. "Oiva" said. The revenant. The scrag. And we went. We walked. I—well, I kept my eye on the scrag. I also let myself drift to one side. It seemed unlikely that a few strides this way or that was going to make a significant difference if this specter, this phantom, this boggy-boe were to fall on us and try to suck the blood out of us—but I couldn't help myself.

"So," the revenant said cheerily, once we were out of ear-shot of the other old men. "They shot me dead, and here I am."

"Here you are, all right," Maiju said. It seemed to me ta was already shaking off the initial dread—finding a calmer place inside. "You recognized us through our disguises."

"How could I not?" it grinned. "I knew you'd be coming along today."

"Oh," Maiju said, ta's voice now with an edge in it—an edge that seemed equal parts fear and sarcasm—"you knew, did you? Dead people know everything?"

"Not everything. Just important stuff."

"Sorry to call you out as Algot—after you thoughtfully gave us Russian old lady names."

"No problem," the scrag said. "These ain't safe times."

"Especially since you published a book under my name. That was kind of you. Putting me in danger too. And J I too, just for living with your pseudonym."

"So sorry about that," it said. "I had no idea it would back-fire the way it did. I just wanted to ride on your coattails a little. Sell some books with the name of a popular author."

"Yeah, it's been some ride, all right."

"Hey, you're still alive, ain't you?"

"Barely," Maiju said.

The revenant put both hands on its heart—or where a liv-ing person's beating heart would be. "I am truly sorry. Please accept my humblest apologies."

"Yeah, yeah," Maiju said. "Of course we accept them. J I? Do you accept my dead friend's apology?"

"Any friend of yours is a friend of mine," I said, trying to control the tremor in my voice. "E-even a dead one."

We walked in silence for a while, processing this new turn of events. In very different ways, of course. My "processing" mainly consisted of struggling to suppress a panicky desire to run away as fast as I could, screaming. Maiju was mainly just irritated, as if someone had thrust a colicky baby into ta's arms and said, "Here, this is yours, take care of it." Ta's main concern was *What are we getting ourselves into, here?*

I looked over at Maiju: *how are you not afraid of this thing?*

Ta's irritation changed to brief amusement: *It's just Algot. I've known him forever.*

Well, irritated amusement. Irritation at Algot, amusement at me. At my panic.

You may have known Algot forever, I thought jumpily, *but this isn't Algot. It's a dead thing.*

Maiju just snorted. Telepathically.

20

The dead thing itself walked between us like an excited little kid, its eyes darting from Maiju's face to mine, registering every detail of our surroundings as we passed. My whole body seemed to be buzzing and fizzing with horror. There was a redness behind my eyes.

"But Algot," Maiju said finally. "Are you quite sure you're dead?"

"Sure I'm sure," Algot said, as if ready to take umbrage. "Why would you even ask that?"

"Because," Maiju said, "I can feel you. I can squeeze your arm—"

"Ow!"

"See? Ghosts shouldn't feel pain. Ghosts shouldn't have bodies that feel real, alive, substantial."

"Well," Algot said with a sly *gotcha* air, "maybe I ain't a ghost."

"Well then, what are you? How can you be dead and standing there talking to us and not be a ghost?"

"Well, maybe you don't know much about being dead," he said archly.

Maiju gave an uneasy barking laugh. "I don't know anything about being dead, obviously."

"Why don't you listen and learn, then?"

"Fine," Maiju said. "Tell us about it."

"Okay, I will. I'm dead. I got pushed in the Gulf of Finland off that damned transport ship and shot up. They got me, the fuckers."

"All right," Maiju said. "Step one."

"Oh, we're counting now, are we? Fine. Let's see. Step two: somebody explains a thing or two to me."

"Somebody?"

"I don't know who it was. Some guy in Deadland."

"Deadland? That's a place?"

"Hell, I don't know what to call it."

"The afterlife?"

"Sure, whatever. Do you want me to tell it, or do you want to keep interrupting me?"

"I want you to tell it."

"Thank you. So this guy tells me we get a transitional stage. Nine months. You know, you spend nine months in the womb before you're born so you get nine months in this limbo state[64] after you die."

"Limbo?"

"I don't know, what would you call it?"

"Fine, call it limbo. So I'm guessing step three is they give you a limbo body?"

---

[64] For "limbo state" Vatanen has *epävarmuuden tila*, lit. "state of uncertainty." For "limbo body" just below ta has *epävarmuuden ruumiillistuma*, lit. "embodiment of uncertainty," and whenever Algot's ectoplasmic body is referred to, it is *(ektoplasminen) ruumiillistuma*—i.e., neither *ruumis* "dead body" nor *keho* "living body."

In English of course "limbo" is both the theological place where innocent souls (like unbaptized infants) wait to be admitted into heaven and, metaphorically, any transitional or otherwise unresolved state of uncertainty—an unexplained delay or deadlock. (It's also the game where you dance under a low bar, which is the only meaning of *limbo* in Finnish.) This makes "limbo" an economical solution in English, collapsing both the theological and the metaphorical places to account for Algot's nine months on earth after he dies; unfortunately, it also loses the humorous jab of Maiju's "embodiment of uncertainty." [Tr.]

"No, step three is they kick me in the ass and say *get outta here, dead man.*"

"Get outta here dead man? That's not very friendly."

"They don't give a shit about being friendly. You're dead. They're dead. Everybody's dead."

"Okay, but how do they kick you in the ass in step three if getting a body is step four?"

"It's a figure of speech, Maiju. Come on, you're a hotshot novelist, you should know about figures of speech."

"Okay, so you don't have an ass and they don't kick you in it. They're just unfriendly and tell you to get out."

"Right."

"Step four: you get fitted with a new body. Or this old beat-up one."

"What are you talking about, beat-up? You see any bullet holes in it?"

"No, as a matter of fact. That's interesting. So it's not like reincarnating you in your old body. They give you a new one that looks just like the old one."

"No, 'they' didn't give it to me. It just materialized."

"'Just materialized'?"

"Are you going to keep yanking my chain about this?"

"No, sorry, I just—you know, things don't 'just material-ize.'"

"In *your* world they don't. But ask a medium; they'll tell you how it works."

"A medium."

"Sure. You know. A spiritualist. Somebody who talks to the dead."

"Have you run into any of those on your way over?"

"One or two, yeah. They told me about it."

"So imagine me completely ignorant about spiritualism. Tell me too."

"I don't have to imagine you. You *are* completely ignorant about spiritualism."

"So it shouldn't be that difficult to imagine, even for a lumber salesman."

"Hey, you're going to start pissing on me, I'll turn around and go rejoin my new buddies on the brick wall."

"Sorry, sorry, it was a joke. I know you have a lively imagination. Go on."

"Okay. So there is this one kind of medium that can exude ectoplasm."

"Exude? Really? How?"

Maiju apparently knew what "ectoplasm" was. I had no idea. But I wasn't about to interrupt.

"The first one I talked to couldn't do it, but she explained it to me and sent me to one who could. This Russian countess. A real babe."

"And did you actually watch the Russian countess do it?"

"Sure did. Grossest thing I've ever seen. If I hadn't been dead I would have lost my lunch."

"So did it actually come out of her?"

"Yeah. She worked herself up into a trance or whatever, collapsed back in her chair with her mouth hanging slack open, and this thick gooey white stuff started foaming out of it. Ectoplasm. After a while it stopped oozing out and the medium came out of her trance. She told me to come over closer, and then started mumbling something. The goo started shaping itself, till it looked more or less like me. I tried to say I was never that fat, or squat, and that wasn't my face, and so on, but she just waved dismissively and said once I got into the material it would take the shape I'd had in life. I asked her how I was supposed to get in there, and she said 'jump.' So I jumped."

"And that was it? All of a sudden you looked like you again?"

"No, it took a couple of hours, I guess."

"And how long does this materialization last?"

"I don't know. The medium said it varies. Sometimes just a week or two, sometimes months. I'm hoping for the whole nine months."

"Well good luck."

"Thanks."

Maiju stopped, and we all stopped. Maiju stood there staring at Algot for a while, all over. Bending closer to look at this or that detail. Squeezing him here and there.

"So can you eat? Do you sleep?"

"I don't sleep, no. But I can eat."

"What happens to the food? I mean, it's all just white goo inside you, right?"

"I don't know. Maybe I've got all the regular innards. Maybe I digest it and excrete the waste."

"You can take a shit?" Maiju asked. "And a piss?"

"Not sure yet," Algot admitted. "But remember what happened to me in Lohja, when that Russian bitch Olga threw acid on me? That's fixed. I'm good as new down there. Wanna see?"

"No thanks, no," Maiju said quickly. "I'm good."

And started walking again, bent over. I thought I heard ta grumble *dead men, sheesh.*

19

Months passed. The White Terror raged all across the southern parts of the country. We may never know the exact number of victims. Of the two groups that were keeping a tally, the parish record-keepers of the Finnish Evangelical-Lutheran Church and the Finnish Social Democratic Party, the former tended to log uncertain cases as killed in action, the latter as executed. Best guess at this writing in 1922 is that by the first anniversary of the declaration of independence,[65] when Regent Svinhufvud declared a general pardon for "treason,"[66] nearly ten thousand Reds or suspected Reds had been executed at gunpoint, nearly two thousand had vanished without a trace, and more than eleven thousand had starved to death in prison camps. Compare that with the less than six thousand killed in action.

The internal battles among the victorious Whites over what to do with the nearly eighty thousand Red prisoners raged for months. Should we just execute them all and be done with it? That was the opinion of many, and many guards acted on that impulse. Should we just let them all go? That was

---

[65] I.e., by December 6, 1918. [Tr.]

[66] This was a blanket pardon, designed to protect both the Reds who had fought in the war (or supported the cause in other ways) and the Whites who had perpetrated the Terror. No White was ever put on trial for war crimes. [Tr.]

unthinkable. The final decision was to consider each case individually, and meticulously. A few were indeed released or executed on the basis of the resulting decisions, starting in September. But the process was so slow, and food was so scarce, that death by starvation was rife. The figures I've seen aren't necessarily reliable, but they say six to seven hundred prisoners starved to death in May, nearly three thousand in June, more than five thousand in July, two thousand in August, and another one thousand in September.

A lot of the soldiers fighting on the Red side were crofters. I wasn't able to travel to Ostrobothnia to check on my family until much later, the summer of 1919, after Algot and Maiju and Irmari were gone; I found my mother still alive, but not many other members of the crofter families I knew. My father had been shot one night by a posse of angry landowners who were rampaging through the village, taking "revenge" against crofters for the war. Many very young boys had been shot too—the boys who had been too young to fight in the war, including some newborn male infants. My mother told me of Red Army "recruiters" pressing crofters' sons into battle at gunpoint, many of them fourteen- and fifteen-year-old boys. Almost none of them came home. Those who weren't killed in action mostly died in the White Terror after.

18

One day in August Maiju was shopping in Market Square, in ta's old lady garb, and a familiar voice hailed ta from behind: "Praskovya!"

This time Maiju was prepared: ta turned and greeted Algot Untola as "Oiva."

Get away from him, I cautioned. *He's bad news.*

Don't be ridiculous, Maiju scoffed. *He's harmless.*

Humph, I thought.

"You have a new disguise," Maiju said, indicating the revenant's tailored pin-striped suit and slicked-back hair.

"Oiva Kairamo is coming up in the world," the scrag beamed. "He's the proud owner of the Oiva Kairamo Hedge Fund and Clairvoyancy Parlour."[67]

---

[67] This is not only obviously fiction, but irrefutable evidence that the novel was not written in the early 1920s. The term "hedge fund" derived from what the sociologist Alfred Jones called a "hedged fund"—in 1949. [Tr.]

The first hedge fund to trade on futures was founded in 1920 by Benjamin Graham and Jerry Newman. [Au.]

But this novel claims Algot Untola founded a *hedge fund* in 1918. That obviously would not have been possible. [Tr.]

It's a *novel*. It is fiction. It doesn't pretend to be true. [Au.]

What are you talking about? You present it as a *memoir of your life*. Of course you're pretending it's all true! [Tr.]

Be that as it may, I could have known about hedge funds in 1921 or 1922. [Au.]

"What, you speculate on hog futures and read palms too?"[68]

That company that Warren Buffett called the first hedge fund was not, however, *called* a hedge fund yet—it couldn't be, because the term "hedge fund" had not yet been coined. It was called the Graham-Newman Partnership. [Tr.]

That's all fine and good, but futures exchanges are a lot older than that. The Code of Hammurabi (written in Mesopotamia around 1750 BCE) spelled out the terms of the first derivatives market, built around forward and futures contracts. In the *Politics* (written between ca. 335 and 323 BCE) Aristotle describes a poor philosopher named Thales who offered local olive-press owners contracts whereby he would deposit money with them in advance of the harvest in exchange for a guarantee that would give him exclusive use of their presses at harvest time. This was attractive to the olive-press owners because it allowed them to *hedge* against the possibility of a weak harvest; and it was attractive to Thales because it drove up demand and allowed him to sell his future-use contracts to other growers at advantageous rates. Really all that Algot Untola or Countess Kravatskaya would have had to do to get the idea for their hedge fund would have been to read Aristotle. Surely not a stretch. [Au.]

What Thales created was really more like an option contract than a futures contract, because Thales wasn't forced to use the presses if the harvest was poor. [Tr.]

Okay, but what about the futures exchange opened at the Dojima Rice Exchange in Osaka, Japan, in 1710, two centuries before Algot Untola? Or the London Metal Market and Exchange Company, founded in 1877, four decades before? [Au.]

Okay, but this novel isn't set in Osaka, or London. It's set in Helsinki. What you wrote in Finnish was "Kairamon Hedgerahasto ja Selvänä-kösali." Not only would *hedgerahasto* have been an impossible term in Finland before the 1970s; a *hedgerahasto* in Finnish is a fund, a pot of money, not an investment company, which is what a hedge fund is in English. [Tr.]

I've got this fund that I sit on. Why don't you kiss it. [Au.]

Oh, real mature. [Tr.]

[68] So Maiju immediately knows what a hedge fund does—in the English-speaking world? This complicated form of financial speculation, which 99% of native speakers of English in the twenty-first century don't understand, is instantly transparent to a Finnish novelist and actor (not an investor) in 1918 like Maiju? [Tr.]

"Not hogs yet, no," the thing said modestly. "That's next. So far just poultry futures."

"What poultry?"

"Chickens, ducks, and pigeons."

"How is there a futures market for pigeons?" Maiju wondered, gesturing around at all the squab-on-the-hoof pecking at trash across Market Square.

"You'd be surprised," the revenant said with a creepy smile. "And I'm not the clairvoyant. My girlfriend is."

"Oh, you've got a girlfriend now?"

"Sure do. And my restored parts are working like a charm."

"I don't want to hear about your parts," Maiju said.

"We do it seventeen times a day."

"Seventeen!"

"Count 'em. Once every hour on the hour. My girlfriend's hot to trot."

"Those parts that I don't want to hear about must be getting tired."

"Never. That's the great thing about being dead. No impotence."

"Well, that's—disgusting, but whatever. So how old is this girlfriend of yours? Eighteen?"

"I'm not sure. She says she's forty, but I suspect she's a lot older than that."

"So this is geriatric sex you're bragging about here."

"For me, sure," the dead thing laughed. "For her, necrophilia."

"Eww!"

"Tell me about it," it said, still laughing. "But hey, what are you doing right now? Come back to the office and meet my girlfriend."

"What's her name?"

Oh, get over yourself. [Au.]

Both of you, grow up. [Ed.]

"Countess Nina Kravatskaya. She's a Russian avant-garde spiritualist. She hates the Bolsheviks."

"I bet," Maiju said. "And I'm sure the feeling is mutual."

"You'll love her. Come on. See what I've got going on these days."

Maiju dithered for a moment.

Surely you aren't seriously considering— I began.

And that seemed to settle it: "Sure, I'll come," Maiju said to the thing. "Where's your office?"

"In the Stock Exchange building, a block north of the Esplanade."

"Oh, that's close. Just let me buy these potatoes first."

So they traipsed the two blocks along North Esplanade to Fabianinkatu and turned right. There on the next block was the Stock Exchange, which the living Algot Untola had been defending, in a way, almost exactly a year earlier. They walked along the gray granite façade, then turned in through the entrance and walked up the stairs to the second floor, where Algot opened an office door on the central corridor about halfway down. The sign above the door did indeed read Oiva Kairamo Hedge Fund and Clairvoyancy Parlour. Maiju could hear voices through a heavy red velvet curtain on the right side of the office: Countess Kravatskaya, presumably, with a client.

"Take a seat, take a seat," the dead speculator urged. "Nina will be finished with her reading soon. It doesn't sound like a séance."

Maiju sat.

"So tell me about this," ta said. "How does a dead guy put an operation like this together in, what, a month? Two months? Probably the countess's money?"

"No, she was living hand to mouth when I met her. But you know, she does the whole ectoplasm thing, barfs it right up. You remember, she's the one made me this body in the first place. And she's certainly the brains behind the operation. She harked up a heap more ectoplasm, let it harden, then started slicing off these paper-thin slices. She had a special slicer made. We cut them into the right size for Finnish marks, and transformed them into thousand-mark bills."

"You knew how to do that?"

"Nah. I did it. Nina couldn't do it on her own, but she taught me how."

"So now you speculate on the futures market."

"Right. And what better job for a dead guy who not only knows the future but is tearing up the sheets with a clairvoyant?"

"So but a hedge fund speculator and a spiritualist don't usually open an office together. Don't clients on both sides of the curtain find it a little—strange? Unnerving, even?"

"Not at all. They love it. Nina gives me credibility because she knows the future, and I give her credibility because I'm this rich capitalist tycoon."

Maiju shook her head in wonder. Back in our apartment I was shaking my head and grimacing with repugnance.

About that time the spiritualist reading ended and out walked Senator Oswald Kairamo—the very man who had demanded that the Director of Viapori Prison execute Algot Untola (or was it Maiju Lassila). I couldn't believe it. Wouldn't he *recognize* the revenant as Algot Untola? Wouldn't he realize that this man standing before him had either survived his supposed execution, or—unthinkable, I know—come back from the dead?

But no: the senator stepped up to the dead thing in a friendly manner, stuck out his hand, and said "Cousin, thanks again."

Cousin?

"Cousin," the revenant said in the same bluff hearty tone, "you're entirely welcome. Come back any time!"

And the senator opened the door into the corridor and was gone.

"Cousin?" Maiju too now said.

"Yeah, funny, isn't it?" Algot smiled. "The guy who so desperately wanted me dead thinks I'm his long-lost cousin!"

"He didn't recognize you as Algot Untola?"

"The only time he ever laid eyes on Algot Untola was on that transport ship. I'd been beaten black and blue and was in chains. Now look at me."

"And you knew he wouldn't recognize you?"

"I suspected it."

"And I guess you must have been planning this, because when we met you on Katajanokka you were already calling yourself Oiva Kairamo."

"Well, quite," Algot said. "I told you I'd met Nina, and she had—"

And at that moment the countess herself emerged through the red curtains. She was a short, wiry, compact sort of woman with a tight head of black hair who did indeed look about forty.

"Oiva," she said in Russian, "you have a guest?"

"Yes, Nina," the scrag said, also in Russian, "I'd like you to meet an old, old friend of mine, the novelist Maiju Lassila. We knew each other back in Tohmajärvi. Ta's a few years younger than me, but has to walk around disguised as an elderly Russian woman to hide out from the White Terror. Maiju, or should I say Praskovya, Countess Nina Kravatskaya."

"Oiva," the countess said, instantly angry, "you need to tell me about your friends before I give readings."

"What?" "Oiva" said, eyes wide.

"Maiju Lassila was on a list the senator gave me. He wanted to know where he could find those people."

Suddenly it seemed the air had been sucked out of the room.

"Nina—what did you tell him?" the revenant asked carefully.

"The truth, as far as I could suss it out from my sources in the afterlife. That they had all fled to Russia."

"Maiju too?"

"None of those spirits had ever heard of Maiju Lassila," the countess said. "*I* had never heard of Maiju Lassila, thanks to you." She gave "Oiva" another withering glare, but then turned to Maiju with something approximating an apologetic look. "Sorry."

"Hey, that's fine with me," Maiju said.

"So did you tell him that Maiju had fled to Russia too?"

"I did. Seemed like the most economical thing to say."

"Well," the dead speculator said, exhaling with relief, "no harm done, then. That was quick thinking, Nina. Sorry I didn't tell you about her, but you handled it perfectly." He looked down at the countess's hands. "Did he leave the list with you?"

She nodded. "Let me get it." She brought it back. Together the countess and Maiju peered over the revenant's slim shoulders as it read out the names:

"Tuomas Hyrskymurto, Väinö Jokinen, Ferdinand Kettunen, Otto Wille Kuusinen, Maiju Lassila, Konsta Lindqvist, Kullervo Manner, Eino and Jukka Rahja, Irmari Rantamala, Yrjö Sirola, Juho Sainio, Juho Viitasaari.[69] Well," he said, with

---

[69] The non-heteronym names on this list were high-ranking members of the Finnish Communist Party or (like Juho Viitasaari, 1891-1920) top officers in the Red Army; all of them except Maiju and Irmari had fled Finland to Russia at the end of the war. All of the names except Maiju and Irmari were also on a hit list designed for a raid on the Kuusinen Club on August 31, 1920; the only survivors of that hit were Kullervo Manner (1880-1939), Eino Rahja (1885-1936), Yrjö Sirola (1896-1936), and Otto Wille Kuusinen (1881-1964). They happened not to be in the club at the time of the raid. O.W. Kuusinen is especially interesting not only because he survived that hit but because he lived until 1964; the other three died in the thirties, of tuberculosis (Manner and Rahja) or an aneurysm (Sirola), but more generally of Stalin's Terror, branded enemies of the people, as in fact were almost all the Finnish Communists then working in the Soviet Union. Kuusinen was an extraordinarily rare exception. He chaired the Finnish Social Democratic Party in 1911-1913 and later was a long-time high-ranking officer of the Finnish Communist Party; in the Soviet Union

a wry look over his shoulder at Maiju, "you're in good company. A bunch of Red politicians and officers—and you and Irmari."

"Well," Maiju said, "at least we now know that the disguise is still necessary."

"Yeah." The scrag looked solemn for about ten seconds. Then he had a thought that brightened his face. He beamed back and forth between Maiju and the countess. "But hey, how's about we go get us some lunch at the Club? The three of us. The Stock Exchange Club, right here in this building. I'm friends with Julius Tallberg and trade councilor Victor Ek, the guys who created Aktiebolaget Börs[70] eight years ago. Oh, also with Lars Sonck, their architect who designed this building. I had to buy stock in the corporation to get Nina and me memberships in the Club, but it's worth it. It's a great space. You'll love it. Say you'll join us!"

"Oiva," the countess said with an edge in her voice, tapping her watch face with an index finger, "aren't you forgetting something?"

"Oh, right, sorry, it's that time again, isn't it!" cried "Oiva," with what seemed to me rather perfunctory delight. "But listen, Maiju, I mean Praskovya, we'll be ten minutes, fifteen tops. Please make yourself comfortable while you wait."

"No, no, sorry," Maiju said quickly, "I can't stay, I have— there's a place I need to be right now, I'm late already."

---

he was also a high-ranking Party officer and member of the Communist International. Finns today remember him as the leader of the puppet Terijoki (or "Kuusinen") government installed by the Soviet Union during the Winter War, 1939-1940. The idea was that once the Soviet Union annexed Finland, as they had recently annexed Estonia, Latvia, and Lithuania, Kuusinen's government would run the new People's Republic. It didn't quite work that way; Finland fought back successfully. [Tr.]

[70] The official Swedish title ("Bourse Inc.") under which the Helsinki Stock Exchange was originally incorporated in 1910. [Tr.]

"Oh," said the phantom, visibly disappointed. "Well, could you come back after your appointment? We'd love to show you the Club. It's beautiful."

"Some other time," Maiju said, and, vigorously shaking hands with them both, beat a hasty retreat.

17

It seemed the revenant had some kind of recurring need to meet with Maiju, have a brief chat, catch up. I didn't understand it, but then I didn't like anything that dead thing did, so please don't expect to make sense of its comings and goings from my take on it. It seemed to sense that I didn't like it, though, didn't want to share any kind of space with him, so it kept finding Maiju out in the world when I wasn't around.

"Oiva," Maiju would typically say when it hove into view, "how's death?"

"Can't complain," it would say. "Still getting my ashes hauled like clockwork. Ashes to ashes!" It always enjoyed the hell out of this joke. Would chortle richly. Followed by: "Ask me about my business."

"Right," Maiju would say, rolling ta's eyes. "Tell me, Oiva: how's business?"

"Going like gang-busters," it would invariably say. "I've expanded again."

"Oh yeah?" Maiju would sigh. "Tell me about it."

So this one day in early October, on a rainy day with that telltale winter chill in the air, with the wind was blowing right through the cracks in the walls and the ill-fitting window frames, I sat at home in Rööperi wrapped in a blanket, nursing my existential dread, feeling the life-force being slowly exsanguinated from my shivering body while the revenant explained cheerfully that it had expanded from hog futures to publisher futures.

Maiju squinted over at him, thinking *oh shit, here we go again.* "Publisher futures?"

"Sure. My hedge fund now allows publishers—mostly editors, I suppose, but also managing directors and so on—to hedge their own death or disability."

"What, like life insurance?"

"A little, sure. Except that instead of them paying me premiums and their estates collecting benefits if they die, I pay them a lump sum, and if something drastic happens to them before the set date, I lose my investment."

"Which doesn't hurt you, since you're playing with funny money."

"Right you are!"

"So in a way you're giving them a sense of false security."

"That's one way of looking at it, yes."

"And also, coincidentally, giving potential assassins a little nudge."

"Oh, now wait," Algot protested. "How do you get that?"

"Presumably you've put the word out that these people have hedged their deaths."

"Well ..."

"Of course you have. And anyone who hates those publishers hears about the hedge and thinks, 'That bastard thinks he's safe, he's hedged his death, but guess what ...'"

"Yes, I suppose that could conceivably happen," the scrag said—and a smile tugged at the corners of its mouth.

"And don't I vaguely remember you telling me that some of your publishers were on board the transport ship when you were dumped in the drink and filled with bullet holes?"

"I might have mentioned something like that to you, yes ..."

"Who were they, exactly?"

"Just two, actually. Eino Railo and Kyösti Wilkuna."[71]

---

[71] Eino Railo (1884-1948) was a writer, literary scholar, book reviewer, and publisher. He worked as a journalist at two different papers before becoming managing director of Kirja ("Book") Press in 1914, in which capacity he published four of Algot Untola's novels, one under the Irmari Rantamala heteronym and three under the Maiju Lassila heteronym. Railo, who was not only on board that transport ship but on the Market Square shore when they fished the writer's shot-up body out of the water, reported that Untola had jumped into the water himself, and the guards had shot him to prevent his escape. Four years after Untola's execution, in 1923, he published the first biography—and thanatography—of the dead writer, psychologizing the dead man's exclusive reliance on pseudonyms as a product of an unhappy childhood, out of which he never grew. There he read "Irmari Rantamala's" 1909 novel *Harhama* (which he didn't publish) as "the confession and self-revelation of a spiritually and physically sick and generally strange person who had suffered shame and bitter humiliation and been shocked out of his mental equilibrium." He blamed Untola's "unruly and unbridled nature" for the "signature disorientation and inability to develop a train of thought coherently, combined with a murky zealotry" that made him write for leftist papers.

One of the writers on whom Railo later published literary criticism was Kyösti Wilkuna (1879-1922), who was also the editor at Kansa ("People") Press that published the big 1909 books (*Harhama* and *Martva*) that Algot Untola submitted under the Irmari Rantamala name and six novels that he submitted under the Maiju Lassila name, including "her" most popular one, *Borrowing Matches*, in 1910. He also rejected a novel manuscript that Untola submitted under the Liisa Vatanen name, "Veden haussa" ("Fetching Water"). After publishing a poem in 1913 calling for "war and bloody clothes," Wilkuna underwent training as a Jäger or Ranger in Germany and returned to his home region in 1915, where he was ratted out to the Russian authorities in 1916, and spent eight months in prison in Petrograd. He was released during the February Revolution in 1917 and upon his return to Finland became a White activist and Civil Guard organizer. During the war he played a significant role in the White Terror, joining "field courts" that sentenced Red prisoners to death and executed them. After the war he joined the Aunus Volunteer Army in an unsuccessful attempt to "liberate" parts of eastern Karelia from the Soviet Union; soldiers who participated in those "tribal wars" (*heimosodat*) were called "tribal warriors" (*heimosoturit*). His 1922 suicide followed two or so years of escalating mental illness.

"I see. And is it just possible, say by coincidence, that both of those publishers have now hedged their own deaths by accepting a paltry sum from the Oiva Kairamo Hedge Fund and Clairvoyancy Parlour?"

"I'd have to check, but somehow I suspect that ..."

"That you somehow managed to overcome your antipathy toward them and sold them on the idea of hedging their deaths."

"Well, yes ..."

"But didn't they recognize you? Surely you would have met your publishers in person?"

"Never."

"Never?"

"Never as publishers. They were on the transport ship too, of course."

"You never met a single publisher?"

"Nope. I always corresponded with them. Exclusively. As one great writer once described the publisher's view of the author, I was 'an invisible point from which the books came, a void traveled by ghosts, an underground tunnel that put other worlds in communication.'"[72]

His brother's son Kustaa Vilkuna (1902-1980) and Kustaa's son Asko Vilkuna (1929-2014) were both noted Finnish ethnologists. I attended Asko Vilkuna's lectures at the University of Jyväskylä in the spring semester of 1975, and a couple of years later he hired me to translate an article of his, "The Story of the Birch-Bark Strip," into English. Upon Kustaa's death in 1980, Asko's ethnology department hired me again, to translate a book his father had written, *New Times for the Old House*. The "old house" in the title is the one in Nivala in which Kyösti, Kustaa, and Asko were all born. [Tr.]

[72] The "great writer" quoted here is Italo Calvino, who was born in 1923, five years after the events in this chapter and one year after the supposed writing of the memoir-novel. The quotation in the Finnish original is taken from Jorma Kapari's 1983 Finnish translation of Calvino's 1979 novel *Se una notte d'inverno un viaggiatore, Jos talviyönä matkamies*; in my translation I have used William Weaver's 1981 English translation *If on a winter's*

"'Traveled by ghosts.' Cute."

"And I never wrote to them as Algot Untola. I wrote as, well, Irmari Rantamala. Or as—um, Maiju Lassila."

"Oh. Great. This just keeps getting better and better."

"They don't know what *you* look like either," the revenant cried, all innocence, "obviously."

"That makes me feel so much better about all this."

"Sorry…" The dead thing mused for a moment—long enough for a sudden traumatic certainty to rush through me, and as quickly out again, into oblivion, that Algot Untola in life might have written as J I Vatanen as well. "You know," he went on, "I only wrote one thing my entire life under my own name. My Apology. You know, like Socrates when he was condemned to death. Once they'd told me I'd been convicted of treason and sentenced to die by firing squad, I wrote a speech. They never let me give it, the White fuckers. But I wrote that earnestly, as Algot Untola. I wrote 'When I die I know I'll be dying innocent, for I know that I meant well. I have sought to bring peace, to prevent cruelty, I've begged the workers to avoid cruelty and revenge and that's what I've written.'"

"And yet," Maiju said with a light sprinkling of acid, "isn't this whole posthumous financier career of yours just one big unnecessarily elaborate revenge scheme?"

"Oh, now come on, that's going too far."

"How is it going too far?"

"Well, it's also providing a good living for Nina …"

"Yeah. It's doing that." Maiju shook ta's head. "But now tell me, your 'cousin,' Oswald Kairamo, who was in the countess's clairvoyancy parlor that time, looking for me and some others—wasn't he on the transport ship as well?"

"Well, yes …"

---

night a traveler. This is, obviously, another of several flagrant anachronisms that undermine the assumption that this novel was written in Finland in the early 1920s. [Tr.]

"I'm thinking maybe your next diversification move will be into senator futures?"

"I confess, the thought had crossed my mind."

"Algot, you never cease to amaze me."

The scrag in its makeshift body just shrugged and smiled. That smile cut through me like suicide.

16

In late October Maiju began to experience excruciating pain all over ta's body. Or not exactly all over. It was oddly specific: fist-sized blossoms in ten places on ta's body. But the pain in those spots radiated out, so that it felt like Maiju's whole body was in pain. I counted, as Maiju pointed: one on the neck; one, two, three, four on the shoulders and chest; one, two on the lower back; one on the left hip; one, two on the right thigh. Maiju tried to tough it out, but several times a day ta would cry out at a sudden stabbing pain, and once ta simply collapsed in a heap on the floor, wracked and writhing and howling with pain. I urged ta to see a doctor, but ta said it would be too dangerous, and surely, ta added, the pain would pass.

I agreed, of course; but I hated to see my friend in such pain.

Maybe M might know a doctor who would treat you without endangering you, I suggested.

Maybe.

But a week and a half went by without respite—and without M.

Then, late one evening, there came a knock on our door.

M, Maiju thought. *Finally.*

You stay put, I urged. Maiju was lying on the sofa, trying not to writhe. *I'll get it.*

At the door, though, was not M but the ecto-phantom.

"Maiju," he said from the entry hall, "how are you feeling?"

"I've felt better," Maiju replied.

I vacated the living room at this point. I still didn't want to be in the same room with the scrag. I repaired to my bedroom, shut the door. I could hear their conversation just fine, through the walls or through Maiju's mind, I'm not sure which.

"It hurts all over, doesn't it?" the thing said, walking over to the sofa.

"H-how did you know?"

"A little bird told me," it smiled.

"What little bird? I haven't told anyone but J I."

"A dead one," it said.

"Oh."

"It's phantom pain," it said.

"It's what?"

"Phantom pain. People who have a limb amputated can start feeling pain in the amputated limb. The one that isn't there any more."

"But I haven't had anything amputated," Maiju said. "Everything's ..."

"I know," the phantom said. "This is different."

"Different how?"

"I have the same pains. In the same places. Diminished, because this ain't flesh and blood. I don't have nerves. I don't have a nervous system."

I half-expected Maiju to raise one skeptical eyebrow, the way ta always did. But of course the pain was driving ta beyond all skepticism: "What are you—"

The revenant touched every place on his body where it was feeling the diminished pain.

"Right?"

Maiju nodded. "But—"

"They're my bullet holes. Those are the entry wounds for the bullets that killed me. I'm feeling them again now, in this ectoplasmic body. This phantom body. It's a whole new meaning of phantom pain, of course, since I am myself one big phantom!"

"So—" Maiju began.

"I know what you're going to ask," it interrupted. "No, phantom pain normally has nothing to do with actual phantoms like me. The amputees don't have ectoplasmic prostheses. They have *nothing*. Just air. They feel the phantom pain out in the air where the old limb used to be. It's like a virtual limb. I'm special."

"No," Maiju said impatiently. "Listen to me. What I was going to ask was, what does any of this have to do with me? I'm not a phantom, and I don't have a phantom body, and my body is not *your* phantom body. How can I be feeling *your* phantom pain?"

"Well, that's the mystery," the thing said. "I assume, though, that it has something to do with me publishing that novel under your name. I projected myself onto you in life, so now you're feeling what I feel in death." It stopped. "Something like that," it added, looking sheepish. "I know it sounds hare-brained."

"Yes, it does," Maiju said firmly. "But what the hell, everything else about you coming back to life these last few months has been equally hare-brained, so why should this be any different."

"You might have a point there," it nodded.

"My question, though, is what I'm to do about it? I can't live like this. I'm in constant excruciating pain."

"I'll send M around," the revenant said.

"You know how to get in touch with him?"

"Of course! I'm dead, remember?"

Maiju tossed ta's head a little. No patience for "Oiva's" dumb dead jokes.

It left soon after. The very next morning, though, early,

before dawn, M knocked on the door. Had a doctor with ta. The doctor prescribed laudanum, one teaspoonful every three hours. He had a bottle of it with him, and poured the first dose into the teaspoon M had put in Maiju's hand. The effect was almost immediate. Maiju began to relax the muscles ta had been tensing for nearly two weeks; soon ta was feeling euphoric.

"Doctor," ta murmured, as ta sank into an otherworldly reverie, "this is safe, isn't it?"

"Absolutely safe," the doctor said. "We give it to the mothers of suckling babes, to rub on their little ones' gums when they're teething, to soothe the pain."

"Okay, good," Maiju said dreamily—and then drifted into outer space.

15

That evening I went out for a walk. I walked down Iso-Roo-bertinkatu ("Great Robert Street"), which we called Iso Roba, down to Sinebrychoff Park, which we called Koffi Park—up the steps to the right off the street, then along the winding path-ways, enjoying the dark and the quiet. The park was empty, except for a middle-aged man on one park bench—who ad-dressed me by my initials. Damn: "Oiva." The scrag.

"Sorry, J I," it said. "I know you don't enjoy being this close to me. But I have a favor to ask. Agree, and the time you spend in my proximity will be very short, I promise."

"All right," I said heavily. "What is it?"

"I'm wondering whether you might conduct an interview for me."

"Who would I be interviewing?"

"One Sten Lille. A sea captain."

"And what would I be asking him?"

"I have been able to determine that he captained the trans-port ship taking me to Viapori for execution."

"Ah."

"I'd like to know as much about that trip as possible."

"Of course you would."

"Yes. Especially, I suppose, the name of the man who pushed me into the water."

"So you can have your revenge."

"Perhaps. We'll see. Will you do it?"

"I suppose. How will I find him?"

"I have his address." The scrag handed me a piece of paper. "As far as I can tell, he doesn't have a telephone. But if you could go to this address tonight, you might find him in. If he's out, you might be able to ask someone where to find him. In what bar, I would assume."

"Fine. How shall I report back to you?"

"I'll find you." The revenant's fake face made a smile-like contortion. "I'm quite good at that."

The captain lived in a basement apartment in Kaisaniemi. I found him home.

"Yes?"

He'd been drinking, but as far as I could tell was not yet in the bag.

Should I give him my real name? Maybe not. I tried to remember the name of the writer in Maiju's *Love* novel.

"My name is—Artturi Turonen," I said. "I represent the Sailors' Pension Fund, and I'd like to ask you a few questions."

"In the middle of the night?"

"Yes. Sorry for the inconvenience."

"Uh—all right. Come in, please."

A single candle burned on a low table. Captain Lille motioned me to a chair and I sat. I felt some subtle movement over by the window to my left, but it was too dark to see anything; I assumed it was a curtain moving.

"What kind of questions?" Lille asked.

"Is it true that you captained the transport ship from Santahamina Prison to Viapori on May 21 of this year?"

"Y-yes, I believe so," the captain said.

"Do you remember who else was on board ship that day?"

"Not really, no."

"You had some soldiers, correct? The execution squad? Or were they waiting for you at Viapori?"

"What is this about? What does this have to do with my pension?"

"Just answer the question, please."

"I want to see some kind of identification."

So this was not going well. I suppose his resistance was to be expected. It must have been a rather controversial trip. But what was I to do? It seemed unlikely that I would get the kind of information out of him that the revenant wanted.

But then a voice drifted out of that place by the window where I had sensed a flutter of movement. A calm voice. Soothing. An elderly male voice.

"Captain Lille," it said in lightly accented Finnish. "Perhaps you could put aside your qualms and give this man the information he needs."

And then a pair of glasses, with the candle flame reflected brightly on each lens, floated up out of nowhere and landed neatly on what I assumed was a person's nose.

"Who are you?" Captain Lille said hoarsely.

"Never mind that," the elderly voice said. "Please, do not be afraid. Just answer the questions."

"All right." The captain's voice now sounded quite subdued, as if hypnotized. "What do you want to know?"

"Did you have soldiers on board?"

"Yes. A supplementary battalion of volunteers. I was a member of that battalion as well. We were to handle the execution."

"This was a supplementary battalion in the White Army?"

"Correct."

"Who were some of the guards?"

"Gunnar Björling[73] was one of them. A poet of some sort,

---

[73] Gunnar Björling (1887-1960) was an experimental (dadaist) poet, one of the great Finland-Swedish modernist writers of the 1920s, along with Edith Södergran (1892-1923), Elmer Diktonius (1896-1961), and Rabbe Enckellin (1903-1974). He was originally a Social Democrat, but switched sides and became a zealous White during the Civil War. Since he didn't publish his first poetry collection until 1922, there is no way Captain Lille

they told me. There were other writers on board too, but they weren't guarding the prisoners. They were just observers."

"What other writers?"

"Um, let's see. Railo. Kaila. Tarvas. Wilkuna.[74] At least those four. There was a senator on board too."

"All Whites?"

"Of course."

"Who were the other guards?"

"Wolmar Henrik Ståhlberg. Let's see. Viljo Numminen.[75] That's all I can think of."

"So what happened to Algot Untola? He somehow ended up in the water?"

"Yes, unfortunate incident, that. The guards had to shoot him right there in the water. I detailed a couple of men to row out and fish his dead body out of the drink. They took it ashore."

"Did he jump into the water, or what?"

"No, he was pushed."

"Who pushed him?"

---

could have called him a poet in 1918—an anachronism that could still be explained if this novel was written in 1922. [Tr.]

[74] We have seen Railo and Wilkuna as publishers, of course—see note 71— but they were also prolific writers. Toivo T Kaila (1884-1961) was a non-fiction writer better known as a high-ranking bureaucrat; from July to November, 1918—beginning just two months after the murder of Algot Untola—he served as Finnish consul to Estonia during the German occupation. Toivo Tarvas (1883-1937) was a novelist who also published two books in 1918 about the war, *Velisurmaajat: "Vallankumous"-romaani* ("Fratricides: a 'Revolution' Novel") and *Tuokiokuvia Helsingin vapautuspäiviltä* ("Vignettes of the Days of Helsinki's Liberation").

[75] Wolmar Henrik Ståhlberg (1887–1940) was later Second Assistant Director of the Turku House of Correction (which in 1924 was renamed the Turku Central Prison). Viljo Numminen (1896–1960) later served as a Justice on the Finnish Supreme Court. [Tr.]

"Wolmar did."

"Wolmar Ståhlberg?"

"Yes."

"Why? That was sort of an odd thing for a guard to do when a prisoner is being transported for execution."

"Yes, I suppose it was. This prisoner, though—what did you say his name was?"

"Algot Untola."

"Huh. I think everybody called him something different. A woman's name, for some reason."

"Maiju Lassila?"

"That's it. I saw the manifest and thought we were going to be executing a woman. Turned out to be a man with a woman's name."

"So you were saying, Ståhlberg shoved him overboard?"

"Yes, this prisoner—this Untola?—I called him Lassila—started taunting the guards. Calling them cold-blooded murderers and traitors and such like. Wolmar didn't take kindly to that kind of talk from a goddamned Red. He lost his temper, told the prisoner to shut up, but the prisoner wouldn't shut up, so Wolmar gave him a shove—oops, right into the drink. So out came the guns, blam blam. Maiju Lassila was dead in the water. I mean—the other guy. Untola."

"So you say you sent a rowboat out to fish the body out of the water?"

"Yes. It drifted fast, but the extra man in the rowboat nabbed it and hauled it aboard. Took it to the Market Square dock."

"Not to Viapori?"

"No. Would have been too far to row. We went to Viapori, left the boat to row to Market Square."

"You couldn't have told the boat crew to bring the body back to the transport ship?"

"Nah."

"Why not?"

"Well. You know how it is."

"No, sorry, I don't."

"A wet bloody mess on deck. Nobody wants that."

"So—taking that wet bloody mess on board would be, what, *unpleasant*?"

"Exactly."

"For whom? The soldiers? Surely they were used to it."

"No, of course not."

"Then who? The observers? They preferred a nice clean death by firing squad?"

"Well ..."

"Or the prisoners? The other poor souls anticipating a similar end in an hour or two. You didn't want to upset them?"

"No, don't be ridiculous. They were Reds, for Christ's sake. Who cared what they felt about it? It was just, you know—an avoidable unpleasantness. Nothing more."

I sat for a moment, digesting that. Then:

"Thank you," I said. "I think that's probably enough. You've been most helpful."

"You'll make sure my pension is safe?"

"Absolutely."

I climbed up out of the captain's basement apartment to find the scrag waiting for me, leaning up against a nearby lamppost. I told it what I had found out. It thanked me and asked whether I'd had any trouble getting the captain to talk. I said I had, at first, but there was a spooky presence in the room that had exerted some kind of mind control, and the captain had let it all come flowing out.

The scrag gave another pseudo-smile.

"Nina told me she would arrange some otherworldly support for your interview," it said. "Glad it helped."

I looked at it, the scrag, the dead thing, and suddenly saw it as a great carrion bird, a man-sized crow, looming black over my prone excarnate body, pulling out of a great gaping hole in my chest long sinewy ropes of entrails like strips of paper with its grisly beak.

Sky burial for one that never was.

14

You may not be entirely surprised when I tell you that Maiju's first drug high didn't last. It was good for an hour and a half of euphoria that first time, and maybe another half hour of ordinary pain-free existence; but as ta came down off that high, the pain started up again, and Maiju soured quickly. M stayed all that first day, making sure Maiju didn't take more than the prescribed dose—which meant an hour of escalating pain for every two hours of relief. Maiju was a good soldier while M was around; but that evening, after M had left, ta began to agitate for the next dose before the full three hours were up. I resisted, but frankly was never any good at resisting Maiju. I was, in any case, almost frantically relieved myself that this pain-killer was working so beautifully. And the doctor had said, hadn't he, that it was absolutely safe?

For several weeks, perhaps a month, Maiju was satisfied taking a teaspoon of laudanum every two hours. The same doctor stopped by every couple of weeks to check on Maiju's condition, and clucked in mild disapproval when ta told him how often ta was redosing. Each time he brought a new bottle and warned Maiju against developing a tolerance to the drug. Maiju asked what that meant; the doctor said "constantly needing more." Maiju assured him that ta was okay with ta's current dose. The doctor said "okay, good," but it was clear that he didn't believe that would last.

I asked the doctor what was in the drug; he said it was a

tincture of opium, "completely harmless." What, I wondered, was a "tincture"? He said it was 10% opium dissolved in ethanol, plus a few other additives, like sugar, saffron, and eugenol. Eugenol? An extract of various essential oils, from clove, nutmeg, cinnamon, basil, and bay leaf. That sounded safe enough.

Over the next month or so, things kept getting worse. Maiju started feeling depressed. The drug continued to ease the pain in ta's body, but the depression began to bite into the euphoric high. More and more ta felt dizzy and nauseated. Ta's mouth was dry now much of every day (and night). Ta hardly ever wanted to eat; I insisted, pushed, until ta got some food down. Ta kept upping the dosage: taking two teaspoonfuls every two hours, then three. Ta needed new bottles of the drug more and more frequently. When M's doctor refused to provide it, Maiju pressured M to get some from another doctor, and then from yet a third.

Maiju's deterioration, I have to tell you, took a severe toll on me. On my sense of reality, I suppose. On my sense of self. Who I was, whether I was anybody at all. I lived through Maiju. I took my whole belief in myself from our friendship. More and more, as the months went by, I felt a kind of panicky dread spreading through me, like a thousand worms.

I even wondered whether Maiju's laudanum could help me feel better as well.

But then I thought: *what "me"?*

On the upside, Maiju's dreams were so vivid, and so strange, that ta began to write again—or at least think about writing. Ta began to plan a big new novel, next to which all ta's earlier books would pale. Ta took copious notes, discussed the emerging conception with me. It would be a fantasy novel, about a mysterious virus that was infecting the entire globe, and killing most of its victims, but also giving them glorious visions of total transformation. If only someone could survive the virus's ill effects long enough, ta could implement sweeping changes in world politics and culture. Those changes would also involve a miracle cure for the virus. The virus was somehow cognizant of these visions, and did its best to kill the visionaries faster, lest it lose its access to hosts and die out; but a small group of visionaries would somehow find a way to fight the virus and begin to implement the necessary changes.

Maiju also envisioned a whole new literary technique, to be developed out of hints in various strange works from the past, like Laurence Sterne's *Tristram Shandy*, Knut Hamsun's *Hunger* and *Mysteries*, Arthur Schnitzler's story "Leutnant Gustl," and some of Anton Chekhov's short stories. The idea would be to go inside characters' minds, follow along with the flow of their thoughts, even if that flow seemed to make no sense to the ordinary reader.[76] The technique would help Maiju tease out of the mental confusion caused by the virus an emergent visionary mindset—but would also allow ta to burrow into the virus itself, imagine and narrativize a viral consciousness as a kind of malignant deity.

---

[76] What Maiju is imagining here, of course, is what Alexander Bain in 1855 and William James in 1890 termed the "stream of consciousness" (also called "interior monologue"). It was in April of the very year in which Maiju envisions it as a narrative technique, 1918, that the British novelist May Sinclair first used the term in a literary context, applying it to Dorothy Richardson's *Pointed Roofs* (1915). James Joyce began using it in *A Portrait of the Artist as a Young Man*, which he began writing in 1907 and serialized in 1914 and 1915; his most extensive use of the technique of course came in *Ulysses* (serialized beginning in 1918, Maiju's year, and published in its entirety in 1922). [Tr.]

13

I confess: in my relationship with Maiju and M I mostly felt like a child. Not necessarily their child; just a child that lived with them. They were only three years older than me, but the class difference weighed heavy on me—and it wasn't just that. They always seemed more mature, more poised, more responsible. They always had money and other resources. I depended on them. It was almost as if they had created me, pulled me out of their mouths or ears. If they had ever suddenly decided that I was a bother to them, or in the way, they would have snuffed me out and that would have been that. I never would have existed.

A disgusting thought: the dead thing had pulled his ectoplasmic body from the mouth of the Russian Countess. And here I was, imagining something like that had happened to me too ... only from the twins ...

For nearly twenty years, however, since the turn of the century, M was a shadowy figure in our little family. The spy, the behind-the-scenes activist, the one who knows things, the one who can get things done. In a sense M was like an absentee parent—one who provides, but erratically. Maiju and I were flatmates and very close friends. We shared everything with each other but our bodies. There were those times when I wanted to be close to Maiju's body, and brought myself into comforting touch. That time in the nineties when I removed Maiju's socks and lifted ta's bare feet onto my bare belly was not a singular event. I resorted to that life-giving intimacy three or four more times a year over the intervening quarter of a century. Sometimes I would lay myself down lengthwise on the sofa with my head in Maiju's lap, ta's free hand stroking my hair as ta read. Sometimes, more rarely, Maiju did the same to me, put ta's head in my lap. We never did hug much, but that happened occasionally. That experimental kiss early in our friendship never recurred.

I felt enclosed in the Lassila twins' magical embrace for twenty-three, almost twenty-four years. They were different from every other living human—and different in precisely the ways that I needed most. It was the greatest honor and greatest pleasure of my life to be included in their world, their family circle.

Now, with Maiju increasingly trammeled up in laudanum addiction, that was all changing. Day by day the magic was being destroyed, trampled, devastated. My calm, understanding, responsible older sibling, whom I loved and admired, was turning into a petulant, demanding, unpredictable child. At the public library one day, searching for books on opium and finding precious little in Finnish, I found a book in English written in the late seventeenth century by one Dr. John Jones, titled *Mysteries of Opium Reveal'd*; according to Dr. Jones, opium brought about a "mopish disposition, decay of parts, and a weakness of memory." That rang true—especially that "mopish disposition." I had to look "mopish" up: *murjottava, mököttävä, jurottava*. Yes, that was Maiju. Most of every day I felt lonely and afraid: afraid of that mopish disposition, lonely because cut off, excluded, banished from Eden. Sometimes I even hated Maiju intensely—hated my beloved friend! The very thought now brings hot tears to my eyes—and, even if I never showed those momentary fits of bitterness outwardly, I was wracked with guilt for giving in to them inwardly.

At first I could still feel Maiju—feel what ta was feeling,

hear what ta was thinking. I could feel ta fighting back; feel ta aching in those spores of pain (I ached in precisely the same places) but also bending under the shame of addiction; feel ta getting angry at the pain and the shame. I could also feel ta apologizing, wordlessly, for ta's helplessness, ta's neglect of our friendship. Ta missed me too.

But then, gradually—I'm not sure how it happened, or even when—our telepathic bond faded. I assume it had something to do with the clogging up of ta's own emotional channels, the gradual shutting down of ta's ability to communicate even internally, let alone externally. Maiju now spent most of every day lying on the sofa; sometimes I would stand for an hour or more just out of ta's sight line, focusing all my mental energy on the lump under the blanket on the sofa, trying to find my way back in through the thickets of addiction. I inevitably failed. There was nothing there. There was no road through. As a result, I could never be sure what kind of mood ta would be in, what kind of reaction to expect from even the most cautious approach.

It felt, in fact, all too sickeningly like the inflamed silences of my childhood home.

12

I have to assume that the revenant got wind—occult wind—of Maiju's literary intentions, because it showed up at our apartment one day in December and started asking about ta. It quickly became clear, though, that the scrag wasn't really interested in Maiju's potential emergence as a brilliant experimental novelist: it wanted to talk about laudanum. Specifically, about Maiju's laudanum addiction.

"You know, of course," it said, as if casually, "that there have been great writers who were laudanum addicts."

"Really?"

"Sure. Thomas DeQuincey wrote a famous controversial book about it. *Confessions of an English Opium Eater.* Wilkie Collins, of *Woman in White* and *Moonstone* fame, started taking laudanum to 'treat' his gout. Actually it didn't treat it; it just eased the pain. He quickly got addicted to it, but fought the addiction for the three remaining decades of his life. It can be done. The really famous one, though, was DeQuincey's buddy, Samuel Taylor Coleridge."

"Coleridge was a laudanum addict?"

"He was. Most of his life, probably. He may have been addicted by his mother, as a small child. It killed him, of course. But he wrote some of his greatest works under its influence."

"Which ones?"

"'Kubla Khan.' 'The Rime of the Ancient Mariner.'"

"Y-yesss ... The dreams. The visions."

"Exactly. But he also wrote *Biographia Literaria* while fighting his addiction. He was hired to translate Goethe's *Faust* into English, because supposedly he understood the demonic better than anyone, and what greater poet was there in English? But he couldn't do it. The laudanum wouldn't let him. He kept on writing, though, and kept on fighting the addiction, for another two decades after giving up on an English *Faust*."

"So I hear what you're saying, Algot. I need to fight too."

"Oh, no, heavens, Maiju—I didn't come to preach! I was just telling some stories about famous writers."

"Sure you were."

"I—"

"Listen. Okay, I heard you. You're worried about me, and want me to fight it. Fine. But tell me how."

"I—" The scrag threw up its arms in surrender.

"That's not really very helpful."

"I have no idea how to help, frankly. Except by telling stories."

"About famous writers."

"Well, yes. People who wrote brilliant books and poems while fighting laudanum addiction. *How* they did it, I don't know. Maybe one of these doctors M brings by can fill you in. I doubt it, though. Those quacks think the damn stuff is safe. Give it to babies."

"But really, Algot, apart from being habit-forming, what is so dangerous about it? You yourself talked about the brilliant visions it gave Coleridge."

"Yeah, but it also gave him mental confusion, muscle weakness, and seizures. *Seizures*, Maiju. Depression. Have you been depressed at all?"

"I—"

"See? Now who's stuck for words?"

Maiju turned ta's head away, lips tight.

"One day Coleridge drank a whole pint bottle of the stuff. A whole bottle. What is that, half a liter? Think: a half liter of laudanum. 10% of that is opium: fifty milliliters of pure opium."

"It's natural ..."

"So is death. Well, not my death, of course. But mortality, that's natural. The fact that we can die. Whether we're shot full of holes in the water or overdose on opiates."

"Look, what do you care? You're out of here in a few months anyway, right?"

"I'm your man from Porlock."[77]

"What does that even mean?"

"I don't want you to go first. The least you can do is slow up a little, wait for me."

---

[77] Coleridge's famous visionary poem "Kubla Khan" is also famously unfinished, according to Coleridge because of an unwanted visitor that he identified as "a man from Porlock." Supposedly he saw the whole poem in an opium-induced dream, and was frantically writing it down, but there came this knock on the door and he lost the vision. There is no hint in that famous story of an addiction intervention, which is how Algot Untola is here reframing it. [Tr.]

11

I decided to call out to M, see if I could reach ta. I had been able to listen in on ta over the years, listen with my whole body, feel what ta's body was doing—but had never succeeded in initiating contact. But I was desperate now. Perhaps M could find someone that knew a therapy for Maiju, or a regimen of some sort, something that would allow Maiju to fight the addiction more effectively, maybe even (I allowed myself to hope) successfully. Dr. Jones said that opium addiction was irreversible—but that was more than two centuries ago. Surely modern science had better methods? Surely something could be done in the twentieth century?

But I couldn't reach M. I tried for days.

Finally, in despair, I turned to the revenant. I still shuddered at the very sight of that dead thing. But I was desperate. I cared more about Maiju than about my own dread of the scrag. I walked to the Stock Exchange building, hoping to find it in. It was out. Fortunately, though, its necrophiliac girlfriend was there, and she was really the one I wanted to talk to. The dead phantom had given Maiju a useless pep talk; maybe the countess could contact the spirits, find someone who knew how to deal with laudanum addiction?

She was snippy with me, but I was beyond caring. She didn't know Maiju. Maiju was Oiva's friend, not hers, and who was I but some tagalong crofter's whelp? The countess and the crofter's kid. Forget about any pride you might have expected me to feel in my accomplishments, my novel, my acting career, my friendship with the most wonderful twins in the world; forget even about any pride I might once have felt in my class-based subservience, my ability to humble myself before the high and mighty, the Counts and Countesses of this world. I had no pride left. I was a wound, begging for a bandage.

To my great surprise, she yielded. She agreed to bandage me up. She led me into the back parlor, through the red velvet curtain I had seen through Maiju's eyes, bade me take a seat. She closed her eyes and began to—rumble. There's no other word for it. Her body moved and sounded like a cart bumping down a hill over a rutted and potholed roadway. Her mouth gaped open and snapped shut, four times, five. She growled, then tipped her head back and howled.

And then stopped. Her eyes popped open.

"*Da*," she said. "*Da*." She looked around wildly. "*Da*," she said again, and continued in Russian: "Yes, I'm looking for a spirit who knows how to cure opium addiction."

She looked straight above her head, then straight across the table, apparently at an invisible being sitting there.

"What? No. No, I don't care about bunion removal. No. No, listen. *Opium* addiction. A *cure*." She drummed her fingernails against the table. Under the table one knee was bouncing furiously.

"These people," she grumbled. "They just ..."

"Excuse me, Countess," I ventured in Russian.

"What?"

"It just occurred to me, Maiju began taking the laudanum to ease the phantom pain in ta's body. Would the spirits know how to remove phantom pain better than they know how to cure opium addiction? They being phantoms themselves, I mean."

Guessing, hoping, that "phantom pain" in Russian was the obvious фантомная боль: *fantomnaya bol'*.

She stared at me intently for ten or fifteen seconds, as if about to scold me for my nonsense Russian. Then turned to the spirits again, all business, in Russian:

"Okay, change of plans. Forget about opium addiction. I know, I know, listen! Listen! I haven't even said what we're changing them to! Well if you're going to talk that way, go, I'll find someone else! Go! No, go! All right, then, stay, but stop being cantankerous! Well if you'd hold your tongue for three seconds I'd tell you! Okay! Here's what we're looking for now! A phantom pain remover. My golden bunny[78] died violently, in pain, and his ectoplasmic body has been reproducing that pain—and now it has passed that phantom pain on to a friend. No, not a girlfriend, I'm his girlfriend! This friend is not a girl, and not a woman. And not a boy or a man either. This friend is just a friend. And ta's in terrible pain. Can anyone help?"

A long wait. I had time to register that she had used the same noun I'd used, фантомная боль—*fantomnaya bol'*. I just had to hope that the spirits knew the word too.

Then the countess seemed to relax—to lean back in her chair and slouch voluptuously.

"Ye-e-e-ss? Ah. Ah, thank you so much. Can you stay close to me for a half hour or so? I'm going to take you to this friend's bedside."

---

[78] "Vatanen's" Finnish here is only slightly less awkward than my English "golden bunny," namely *pupukulta*, which is indeed literally "golden bunny" or "bunny-gold." What makes it less awkward than the English is that *kulta* "gold" is used commonly as an endearment, indeed may be the most common endearment, roughly equivalent in the frequency of its use to "dear." It's used so commonly, in fact, that it can sound neutral, non-endearing, like something you call a person who is technically your dear but is not necessarily all that dear to you. *Pupu* "bunny" and *pupukulta* "bunny-gold" are used, but sound far too sappy for most Finnish adults to address their significant others with. I assume, though, that *pupukulta* here is a Finnish translation of the common Russian endearment зайка золотая ("*zaika zolotaya*"), which is literally "golden bunny" or "bunny (of) gold." [Tr.]

At that, she sat bolt upright, as rigid as a moment ago she was limp, shook all over like a dog coming out of the water, regrouped, and looked over at me.

"Are you ready? Take me to Maiju."

"Thank you, Countess!"

"Don't thank me till we see how this works. You never know with spirits."

We got up and pushed through the red curtains into the outer office, where the scrag was standing. I regulated my reaction: don't bolt screaming. A dead spirit not unlike the revenant just might be able to save my friend.

There was, though, something different about *this* dead thing. This scrag. A qualitative difference. An existential difference. I didn't know how to describe it.

It wasn't just that "Oiva" was loud and annoying. It was—

I didn't know. I couldn't figure it out. It was something that went very deep. Something connected to me at some yawning terrifying place. I wanted to say "the abyss," and balked at my own melodramatic impulse—but I couldn't shake the feeling.

The countess explained the situation to it—to "him." It— "he"—asked whether we wanted h— ... no, wanted *it* to come along, but it was clear *it* didn't want to, so the countess simply said *no* and we walked out.

I couldn't call it "he." I couldn't personalize it.

When we got to our apartment in Rööperi, the countess took over. She explained to Maiju what she was going to ask the spirit to do, and Maiju nodded listlessly.

"Get me a chair," the countess instructed me. I brought one to her by the sofa.

"Draw the curtains," she said next. I did.

Then the rumbling began again, and soon the growling and the howling followed. Then we were in the invisible presence of the spirit again, and the spirit did something, or didn't—who could tell?—and then the countess was saying it was finished, and Maiju should start getting better now. She asked for twenty marks, and I happened to have a twenty-mark bill, and she took it without thanking me and walked out the door.

When I turned back to Maiju, ta was asleep.

10

While Maiju was sleeping, M knocked on the door. I let ta in and beckoned ta into the kitchen so we could talk in low voices without waking Maiju.

Quickly, then, I outlined what I had done—the séance, which purportedly had mobilized a phantom to remove Maiju's phantom pain. I could see M processing this behind a poker face: ta had obviously developed phenomenal skills for regulating and masking emotions over the years.

"Okay," ta said when I was finished. "Let's say what you think happened did actually happen, and Maiju no longer has those intolerable pains. What next?"

"I'm not sure," I said. "But I would think that should make it possible for ta to cut way back on the laudanum, maybe eventually quit using it entirely."

"That would be wonderful, of course," ta said. "But it may be over-optimistic."

"Entirely possible," I said. "That's my desperate hope talking."

"I'm a hundred percent with you there," M said. "What I've read, though, is that it's extraordinarily difficult to quit using opium. It's so hard, in fact, that a lot of countries have already made it much much harder for physicians to prescribe it. Finland is lagging behind, but I've been working behind the scenes—where else, for someone like me?"—ta gave a dry humorless little laugh—"to change that."

"But without the fear of the pain returning—?"

"Even without that fear it's incredibly rare for addicts to get off it. There's this thing I've read about in the foreign medical journals called psychological addiction. Opiates are physiologically the most addictive substances we know; but even a weak physiological addiction is typically also massively supported by psychological factors."

"I don't understand."

"Maiju may be in love with ta's addiction."

"In *love* with it? How can—?"

"I know," M said. "It sounds crazy. Maiju knows how devastating this thing is. But ta may believe that it's also ta's only salvation—the only thing keeping ta sane, say."

"But once ta knows the pain isn't going to come back—?"

"J I, how would Maiju *know* that? Do *you* know it?"

M had me there. I shook my head ruefully.

"For months now Maiju has been killing not just pain but the very possibility of pain. The only way ta could be brought to even test the opposite possibility, that the pain will not return, would be to let the laudanum wear off—wear off even a little bit. And ta's likely to be too afraid to try. We'll see. Ta may surprise us, with superhuman courage. But let's not get our hopes up too high, too soon."

"All right," I said.

"By the way," ta added, "I assume you've been following the posthumous adventures of our old friend from Tohma-järvi, Algot Untola?"

"Yes," I said shortly.

M laughed. "I can see you're not a fan. Nor am I. Anyway, you may be interested to know there have been attempts on the lives of Eino Railo and Kyösti Wilkuna."

"Those are the two publishers?"

"Correct. The ones who came along for the ride to watch Algot get murdered. Execution tourists."

"Gruesome."

"My thoughts exactly," M nodded. "Whatever we think of Dead Algot, these vultures who killed him and now are feeding on his flesh make my skin crawl, and I can't say I'd be heartbroken if somehow they—"

"Got what's coming to them?"

"I was going to say 'met with an accident.'"

"That too," I smiled.

Then a thought came to me.

"You wouldn't, um—know of anyone currently involved on a more or less active basis in engineering that kind of accident, would you?"

Ta laughed. "You mean, am I the attempted assassin?"

"No, no, I—"

"It's okay," M said. "I'm not. And no one I know is. But I certainly don't take offense at you hinting that I might be. I just thought you'd like to know."

"I wouldn't say I'm enthralled by this whole drama," I admitted. "But—"

"I know. There's a certain satisfying rough sense of justice, or sense of rough justice, in a revenge scheme."

"Yes." I thought about that for a moment. "But frankly," I said, "nothing in the world, nothing at all, would give me more satisfaction than Maiju getting off this terrible drug. *Nothing.*"

"Amen to that," M said. Ta looked me up and down. Then extended ta's arms. "Give me a hug."

We hugged. We hugged for a long time. We didn't want to let go.

But then we heard Maiju's faint voice from the living room.

9

M spent the whole day with us. Mostly the twins talked togeth-er. I was happy to stand back and watch. I was a part of the scene. I had made something happen—something potentially transformative, potentially redemptive. Time would tell wheth-er what I had done had worked the way I hoped it had.

M did ask me to tell the story again, of how Countess Kravatskaya and I had sat there in the clairvoyancy parlor talking to the spirits, and how none of the spirits had known how to cure opium addiction, but one had stepped forward claiming to know how to remove phantom pain. How we had walked to Rööperi and created our own satellite clairvoyancy parlor there in the living room, and—something had hap-pened. Maybe.

"You don't know, though, whether anything at all hap-pened," Maiju said out loud.

"No."

"You can't be sure the pain was removed."

"No."

"Well then."

Maiju's tone seemed to say *That's settled, then. No way I'm decreasing my dosage.*

M took over again then, trying to convince Maiju that all it would take would be a *slight* delay in the next dose. Ten minutes. If the pain even hints that it's returning, take the next dose. If there is no pain, wait another five minutes. And so on.

Tiny, insignificant increments of time.

But Maiju was having none of it. "It's not just that the laudanum kills the physical pain," ta said. "It's that not taking laudanum *inflicts* pain."

"But not the same pain, right?"

"Right, but pain nonetheless."

"Think of the benefits, though, of cutting back—of braving the withdrawal pains. You could get your life back. You could write that experimental novel. You could go outside again."

"In disguise."

"Sure, in disguise. Yes. But come on, you're an actor. When did going out in disguise start to bother you? I thought you enjoyed it, in fact."

"I don't enjoy anything any more." Maiju listened to the sound of that. Thought about it. "Well," ta said, "except the laudanum high. That's nice."

"I bet," M said. "The only problem is that it doesn't last forever."

"Right," Maiju said. "And what you're asking me to do is enjoy it less. Less and less. Less often, for shorter periods each time."

"That's it," M said. "Yes. That's what I'm asking. I'm counting on you."

"Counting on me to throw away the greatest source of pleasure in my life?"

"Counting on you to find that place inside you that cherishes more complex pleasures."

"Like what?"

"Like writing. Like talking to J I and me. Like going for walks, going skiing, going skating. Like eating a hot meal. Like drinking coffee."

"That's pretty complex. Coffee, wow."

"Coffee is a hot bitter liquid. The pleasure you used to feel drinking it is *much* more complex than a drug-induced euphoria."

"Whatever."

It wasn't going to be easy.

8

In late December, a few days after Christmas, the phone in our apartment rang. This was a surprise, as it had never rung before—and indeed I had simply assumed it was not connected to the exchange. We had of course been living incognito in the apartment since May; M had presumably been paying the rent, or else ta was working for the organization to which it belonged, and had the use of it; we had had no reason to ask about the phone, or its number, as we had no reason to want people to be able to track us down in the apartment. It seems to me now, in fact, that we still thought of it then as a *telefooni*. The new word for telephone, *puhelin*, had been coined maybe twenty years before, at the turn of the century, and we'd had a working telephone in our Katajanokka apartment; but with all the troubles since then, we hadn't used it much.

I picked up the receiver and said "hello."

An aristocratic male voice greeted me by my initials in German, introduced himself as Baron Uexküll-Gyllenband— the late Ida Aalberg's husband. We had heard that Ida had died a few years before in Petrograd. I could understand spoken German well enough, but was hesitant to speak it, so I replied in Russian; the baron responded with a single word in mangled Finnish: "Key-teh," by which I assumed he meant "kiitos." [79] Apparently Ida had attempted to teach him our

---

[79] "Kiitos" is "thank you"; the baron apparently attempted to use the infinitive "kiittää," to thank, but didn't double the "t" and, as is common among both Russian and German speakers, was unable to pronounce the "ä" (as in "cat"). [Tr.]

language and not made much progress.

He asked me whether he could stop by in a half hour and pick me up; he wanted to ask me something. I wondered for a split second whether this was a trap of some sort, but it was an idle kind of curiosity—not only was I personally never directly in danger of being sought by the police, but M had told us the manhunt for dangerous seditious Reds was pretty much over by early to mid-autumn—so I agreed.

"Pick me up," though? Did he mean in a motorcar?

A half hour later I heard a car horn honking in the street below our window. I looked out and saw the baron standing next to an expensive motorcar, waving up at me in the window. I slipped on my winter coat, hat, and gloves, laced up my boots, and went down.

The baron greeted me like an old friend—a bit condescendingly, perhaps, but then you expect that from an aristocrat.

"Have you been in a motorcar before?" he asked, still in Russian.

"Never," I said, running my eyes over it. It was beautiful— a bright blue. The sun had been up for an hour, and sparkled on the sleek sides of the car and the snow around it.

"Would you like to learn to drive it?"

I didn't respond for a few moments. The question was so extraordinary, at first I couldn't parse it. Could I be sure I had understood the Russian correctly? Водить его: *vodit' ego*, drive him. Drive it: водить автомобиль, *vodit' avtomobil'*, drive the automobile. Surely there was no other conceivable interpretation than that he was asking me whether I wanted to learn to drive the motorcar?

I turned to him. "Yes," I said. "I would love to learn to drive the automobile."

He opened the driver's side door, beckoned me to climb in. I climbed in—feeling like I was entering a magical world.

For the next hour or so we drove around Helsinki. I picked

up the driving fairly quickly, but the baron wanted me to feel entirely comfortable at the wheel.

Finally he had me park the car in front of a storefront, and we got out and went inside. To my surprise, there was an old theater there, in ill repair, but a dozen builders were at work on it, tearing out rotten lath and plaster walls, replacing rotten floorboards, and so on. They had removed all the seats in the house and piled them up haphazardly against the back wall.

"What do you think?" the baron asked, his eyes alight.

"This is your theater," I said. "It's going to be wonderful."

"The Ida Aalberg Theater," he corrected me proudly. "I'd like to invite you to act in it."

I felt the old thrill. It had been nearly a year since I had been in a theater.

"I would be honored to act in the Ida Aalberg Theater," I said.

"But?"

"But I don't know what my legal obligations are to the National Theater."

"That can all be worked out," he said easily.

"All right," I said. "Let's talk with them, see what the situation is."

"Excellent," he said. "And another thing."

"Yes?"

"I need a driver. Would you be interested in working for me in that capacity while the theater is being renovated? Perhaps after as well?"

"Yes," I said, but after a tiny hesitation.

"But?"

"But as you may have heard, my friend Maiju Lassila has been quite ill these last few months. I have been her full-time caretaker." I used the Russian *ee*, "yeyo" [English "her"], echoing the presumed femininity of ta's name, as there is no way of avoiding binary gender in Russian.[80] "I would need to work around that."

"I'm sure we can reach an accommodation," the baron said.

"Good, then."

"You would, presumably, need to go on living with her?"

"Yes," I said simply.

"All right. For now. As part of the temporary accommodation. Eventually, though, it would be most convenient if you were to move into my house on Vironkatu. It is quite spacious. I'm sure you would find it a comfortable place to live."

I thought about that. On the one hand, the idea of no longer living with Maiju was almost unthinkable to me. Maiju was my life—almost literally. I don't know how else to describe it. I still held out hope that ta would break free of the laudanum addiction and resume a normal life. That would give me too ... not just "my" life "back," but a life full stop. I would, as the saying goes, be a real boy. Perhaps Maiju would even join the cast at the Ida Aalberg Theater. Move into the baron's mansion with me.

But I was very tired—tired of taking care of the petulant child ta had become—and, well, also more than tired. I was in crisis of some sort. Existential crisis. It felt like my world was crashing down around me, taking "me" with it. I didn't know whether running away would prevent that; probably it wouldn't.

---

[80] For "her full-time caretaker" Vatanen has *hänen täysiaikainen hoitajansa*, which I would normally (call it "normal," ha) translate as "ta's full-time caretaker"; since Vatanen specifies that the Finnish is a rough translation of the (unavoidably gendered) Russian ta was speaking to the Count, I have rendered *hänen* with "her." A few lines down Vatanen also represents the baron as saying *jatkaa hänen kanssaan asumista*, literally "continue living with ta," but, assuming that that is a Finnish translation of something like продолжать жить с ней/*prodolzhat' zhit' c ney*, I have translated the presumed Russian as "go on living with her." [Tr.]

I wasn't sure I could bring myself to abandon Maiju. Everything in me, or almost everything, rebelled against that.

But the suggestion was weirdly tempting. Almost, I don't know—mystically tempting.

"We can talk about that," I said.

"I'm happy to hear that," he said. "Now, would you mind driving me to the Construction Workers Union?"

7

A few days later, after the new year, M came by again, this time with a guest in tow: a tall stooped elderly man that M introduced as Antti Iisalo. The man was manifestly in considerable pain.

Maiju looked up from the sofa.

"Irmari? You're alive?"

"Barely," the man said. "Hello, Maiju. You saw right through my disguise."

My lord, of course: Irmari Rantamala, M's boyhood friend from back in Tohmajärvi. More recently a controversial novelist and Red agitator—presumably sought by the White police even more frantically than Maiju.

M explained: "Irmari seems to have caught whatever it was you had, Maiju. Intense pain in those exact same spots all over ta's neck, chest, lower back, and legs."

"God," Maiju said. "What are the odds of that?"

"Exactly," M said, then turned to me. "Ta's wondering whether you could take ta to Kairamo's Hedge Fund and Clairvoyancy Parlour for another exorcism."

"'Exorcism'?" I said. "That wasn't—"

"I know, I know," M said quickly. "Exorcism or whatever we want to call it. I told Irmari what you did with Maiju, bringing the countess in, and ta's hoping it might work with ta as well. Get the pain removed spiritualistically, without laudanum."

"Uh, sure," I said, pulling on my boots and warm winter clothes. "No problem."

As we walked, I realized that it was taking every bit of Irmari's concentration not to shriek with pain. I remembered Maiju in that same condition just two months before. I decided it would be better not to try to strike up a conversation, but offered ta my arm. Ta took it gratefully—and I thought I heard ta groan *ahhhh.*

I looked over quickly: ta's mouth had not moved.

And the same voice sounded again inside my head: *you can hear my thoughts?*

Interesting.

Yes, I thought. *And you can hear mine?*

Yeah. Thanks for doing this.

Happy to help, I thought.

I apologize, but I'm afraid I must block you. I need to concentrate on managing the pain.

No problem. Do what you have to do.

And so I began to think about the parallels with Maiju. I could communicate telepathically with both. And those long odds Maiju had mentioned: how on earth could Irmari Rantamala have "caught what Maiju had"? How could that phantom pain possibly be contagious? But of course in a sense Maiju had "caught" it from Dead Algot. Could Irmari have "caught" it from Dead Algot as well? And then the connections started dropping into place: Irmari Rantamala "working" with Algot at *The Workingman* during the war. Was it possible that Irmari was *not* working in that editorial office, but Algot was simply using the Irmari Rantamala name as a pseudonym? Could Algot have asked M to stash Irmari away somewhere safe, like up in northern Finland, far from the killing fields down south? And Maiju had once mentioned that Rantamala had published five novels; perhaps one of them was actually written by Algot and simply published under the Irmari Rantamala name?

If this was in fact the ecto-phantom's phantom pain, could it be that once it was pulled phantomatically from Maiju's body, it had made the jump into Irmari's?

Well, I thought, if this is another victim of Live Algot's lazy opportunism, we'll soon find out the truth.

And sure enough, the scrag was in its office when we got there, and it too instantly recognized Irmari Rantamala. When I repeated M's words that Irmari had "caught" Maiju's phantom pain, it quickly grasped what must have happened, and called the countess out of her parlor.

"We have us another bad case of Red Agitator Phantom Pain Syndrome," it told her, gesturing toward Irmari.

The countess stared at Irmari for about two seconds, then took ta by the arm and carefully led ta into the parlor.

And then it was the scrag and me, just the two of us, occupying that office.

I still wanted to run. My horror at this dead thing had never diminished one iota, in the five or six months since we had first met.

"So," it said, striking a jovial tone, "how's our Maiju?"

"About the same," I said flatly.

It gazed at me for a few seconds. I had no idea what it was thinking. The telepathic link I had with Maiju, and now with Irmari, never did work with the dead thing.

When it spoke, its words were surprisingly blunt.

"You don't like me, do you, J I?"

I considered how to respond to this.

"It's nothing personal," I offered. "I didn't know you well enough when you were alive to like or dislike you."

"You just don't like dead people."

My eyes went wide. So it knew.

"Not the kind that walk around in a makeshift body," I said. "Revenants."

"Fair enough," the thing said. "But what would you say, J

I, if I were to tell you that I created you?"

"I'd say 'never trust a fucking revenant,' excuse my language."

"No worries. We're both men of the world here. Or, well, people of the world. But apart from my being an untrustworthy fucking revenant, do you have any other reason to doubt that I created you?"

"Well, there is the fact that I am sure that my crofter parents created me."

"You're sure?"

"Of course I am."

"You were there when they made you?"

"Well ..."

"You were conscious, and understood the signs of being created by a penis ejaculating in a vagina?"

I'm afraid I blushed at that. I'm not used to people talking that way around me. I suppose the norms of civility are relaxed among the dead.

"Of course you aren't sure. Nobody's ever sure who made them. Did your parents ever tell you they created you?"

"No."

"So you just assume that they must have made you."

"I suppose so."

"Consider another interesting little fact, J I. You are neither a man nor a woman. Right?"

"Right."

"Who else do you know like that?"

"Maiju and M."

"And who else?"

"Um ... Irmari Rantamala?"

"Good guess. And what proportion of the human population, would you guess, is neither male nor female but something other?"

"I don't know. One in five?"

The revenant snorted.

"No. It's anybody's guess, of course, but probably one in a hundred, maybe one in two hundred. It's a relatively rare condition."

I thought about that for a moment. Uncomfortable thoughts.

"And yet—" I began.

"Exactly, J I. Finish that thought."

"And yet a half hour ago four of us neither-men-nor-women were gathered in the same apartment. And two of us had phantom pain that they had, um, caught, or inherited, or something, from you. From your bullet wounds."

"There you go. And how do you explain all that?"

I thought about that. Could I explain it? Could I explain anything, not just in the bizarre afterlife of Algot Untola but my own ongoing life? Did any of it make the kind of sense that a crofter's kid could understand?

"Okay," I said finally—heavily. "I admit the evidence is strongish that you created all four of us. But tell me this: how come M and I aren't writhing in excruciating phantom pain like Irmari there?"

"I don't pretend to understand the cosmological implications of all this, J I, but I assume it has something to do with the fact that I published a novel under Maiju's name and a two-volume novel and a year and a half of *Workingman* journalism under Irmari's name, and never published anything under your or M's initials."

6

When Irmari and the countess emerged through the red curtains, Irmari was the very picture of relief.

Like new? I asked silently.

One hundred percent, ta replied.

The revenant, not being privy to our thoughts, used spoken words: "So I'm guessing the spirit fixed you right up?"

Before Irmari could reply, the countess jumped in with a little history lesson—in Russian: "He was a Russian prince, Prince Yoann Konstantinovich, Yoannchik to his family, son of Grand Duke Konstantin Konstantinovich of Russia, cousin of Tsar Aleksandr III, who of course till his death in 1894 was also King of Congress Poland and Grand Duke of Finland. Yoannchik, as he asked me too to address him, was a gentle, religious young man who was exiled to the Urals by the Bolsheviks in April and in July, along with his brothers and several other royal relatives. He was brutally murdered in a mineshaft near Alapayevsk, a hundred and fifty kilometers from Sverdlovsk. He was thirty-two."

"So his death was as violent as mine," the revenant mused, also in Russian. "He must have encountered this phantom pain problem before." He seemed lost in thought for a moment. "I wonder, did any of his family escape?"

"His widow, Princess Yelena, is languishing in a Soviet prison. Their two children, Vsevolod and Yekaterina, were left in the care of their grandmother, the Grand Duchess Elizaveta

Mavriekievna of Russia, and she was able to escape with them to Sweden."[81]

"Too soon to know whether he passed his wounds on to his children," the ecto-phantom mused further in Russian; then turned to me, switching to Finnish. "J I, how is Maiju? Has ta been able to break free of the opium?"

"No," I said. "Too afraid."

"Maybe if I come back with you," Irmari said, "Maiju would see that the spirit therapy worked, and that ta has nothing more to fear from phantom pain."

"Excellent idea," the revenant proclaimed. "Don't you agree, J I?"

"Sure," I said.

"And I think I'll come along as well. It's time we had a little chat, all of us."

"All of your favorites, you mean," the countess said, somewhat acerbically.

"Yes, dear, if you like. All my favorites. Shall we go?"

---

[81] Prince Yoann (or Johan, or Ivan, or John) was married in 1911. His widow Princess Yelena was held in that Soviet prison for only a few months and then allowed to emigrate; she caught up with her two children, Vsevolod, born in 1914, and Yekaterina, born in 1915, and their grandmother in Sweden, and lived in the Kingdom of Serbs, Croats, and Slovenes (what was to become Yugoslavia) for several years before moving to England. Vsevolod died in 1973 and Yekaterina died in 2007: she was the last uncontested surviving member of the Romanov dynasty (though she renounced her succession rights to the Russian throne in 1937, on the eve of her wedding). Her grandfather Grand Duke Konstantin Konstantinovich was not only the younger brother of British Prince Philip's grandmother Olga, Queen of Greece, but the mediocre poet, dramatist, and Shakespeare translator on whom Vladimir Nabokov based Conmal, uncle of *Pale Fire*'s Zemblan King Charles II. [Tr.]

5

When we walked into the apartment, Maiju was sitting up, blinking in the sun through the window; as we removed our winter gear, ta stood up and walked toward us, slowly, but with a certain determined air.

Maybe there was still a chance?

"Well," ta said, ta's voice echoing the shaky determination I had seen in ta's step, "if it isn't Old Scratch himself."

At first I thought ta meant the revenant, the scrag, and the uncertainty in Irmari's and the dead thing's faces seemed to indicate that they weren't sure either; but then I remembered Nuutti Vuoritsalo's satirical review of *Harhama*, and the same seemed to dawn on Irmari as well, and ta and I both smiled.

"Sorry," Irmari laughed, "I left my serpent and my monkey at home."

"You seem to be feeling better now than you were an hour ago," Maiju said.

"Worlds better," Irmari agreed.

"That dead Russian prince knew what to do," the revenant put in.

Both Maiju and Irmari looked puzzled.

"Russian prince?"

"Wait," the dead thing said. "Irmari, you didn't understand Nina's story?"

"Of course not," Irmari said. "She was speaking Russian."

"You don't speak Russian?" Maiju was incredulous. "How

can you not speak Russian? Even I speak Russian."

"You do?" Irmari said.

"Haltingly," Maiju said. "But yes. Of course. And I understand most of what people say in it."

"Well," the revenant said. "I, ah—I might know something about that."

"Something about what?"

"Irmari's lack of proficiency in Russian. I—well—I once wrote to Eino Railo as Irmari, saying I don't know any Russian."

"But you're fluent in Russian!"

"Of course I am. And in English, German, and French. I always picked up foreign languages easily. I think J I got that from me, in fact."

Everyone looked at me. I blushed. My damn face.

"But," the scrag went on, "I was hiding my identity. I was pretending to be Irmari. What better way than to deny my proficiency with foreign languages?"

"Thanks a lot," Irmari said with mock indignation.

"You're welcome," the revenant smiled.

"I remember wondering about that, though, in fact," Irmari mused. "Railo wrote to me directly, asking whether it was really true that I had no Russian or any other language either, except Finnish, and that even my Finnish wasn't great. If it was true, he asked, how could I possibly have larded my letters to him with so many quotations in not only Russian but English, German, French, and Latin?"

"I always did enjoy messing with that fucker's head," the dead thing said. "You may also remember, though," it added, "that I put out a rumor under your name that you had written the lost third part of *Harhama* in Chinese."

"Chinese!" This was Maiju. "Three thousand pages in Chinese!"

"It was horseshit, of course."

"But," Irmari said, "I do want to hear about the dead Russian prince."

So we told the story the countess had told us, and that led to comparisons of Maiju's and Irmari's pains and their aftermath, specifically Maiju's laudanum addiction and Irmari's complete cessation of all phantom pain. I was cheered to see Maiju taking this conversation seriously.

Well, "cheered" may be the wrong word. "Moved" would be more like it. I had to choke back tears. Maiju saw my emotion, of course, and was moved by it as well; ta reached out a hand and held my cheek for a minute, sympathy and guilt in ta's sweet eyes.

"I'm going to beat this thing," ta said, looking straight into my eyes, but encompassing all the others as well in ta's peripheral vision. "I'm going to fight back. I'm going to decrease my doses until I'm free of it. And I'm going to write. I'm going to write that experimental novel I've been dreaming of. You'll see."

That "you" meant everyone, I suppose; but it was directed at me. I nodded—and then my face crumpled, and the tears sprang out. I couldn't stop them. They flowed freely, and I wasn't ashamed. I loved Maiju, and had missed ta, and wanted ta back. I wanted our life back, the life that we had lived and loved for so many years.

4

And for the most part, ta was as good as ta's word. Ta did progressively cut back on ta's doses, and steeled taself against the withdrawal pains. Sweated profusely. Was wracked with abdominal pain and muscle spasms. Shook uncontrollably. Careened between nervous agitation and depression. Waves of nausea swept over ta.

And of course ta craved the euphoria of the drug high. Misery without the drug, bliss with. What kind of choice was that? Of course the drug high was preferable! And yet ta had sworn to get over it, to kill the craving; ta had looked me in the eye, with ta's sweet hand on my wet cheek, and promised. So ta kept trying. When ta took the decreased maintenance doses of laudanum, ta's hands shook so violently it was difficult to get the drug into ta's mouth. Several times ta got so angry at the shaking of ta's hands that ta hurled the spoon across the room and swilled laudanum from the bottle—and felt wonderful for a while, of course, but also felt bitterly guilty, and resentful of me for "forcing" ta to undergo this ordeal.

There was also the fact that I had "saved" Irmari without laudanum but had not done the same for Maiju. Ta threw that fact in my face several times. I tried to explain, at first, but as my hapless explanations were met with more anger and recriminations, gradually I began to turn a stony face to the accusations.

"You don't care, do you!" was then ta's reading of my stony face.

Sigh.

I also drove for the baron almost every day. He would stop by and pick me up, and we would go out for a few hours, while Maiju tried to write. Upon my return ta would show me the three or four pages of nearly illegible scribbles ta had produced: the withdrawal pains shook ta's body so severely that it was difficult to write legibly. But ta would read them out loud to me, or, if ta was in too much pain to do that, I would labor through the draft, finding a handful of passages to get excited about.

But Maiju didn't accept my trumped-up enthusiasm either.

"Oh, come on, J I, don't pretend. It's rubbish, I know it, and you know it too. Once I kick this damn addiction it's going to take me months to learn to write this novel."

I could only agree. But of course I tried to find convincing ways to be encouraging about these preliminary drafts as well.

"The thing is," Maiju said in frustration one day, "I have no experience writing Literature with a capital L. I'm a popular writer. I'm a folk humorist. I'm not Irmari. I'm not a Symbolist. I'm not a decadent, though of course being addicted to laudanum might qualify me for that."

"And in that *Love* novel of yours you described the Lassila family as having 'degenerated' from a long illustrious past. That's a kind of a hint at decadence, too."

"Sure, but I did it humorously. Parodically. I made it clear that I was taking the piss out of that whole decadent tradition. I was playing with literary traditions, but right up on the surface of the books, having fun with the whole notion of being a writer, writing Literature, winning praise from the critics and the scholars. *Love* was a send-up of the sentimental love story, but more generally of story-telling at large, and the absurd impulse to raise story-telling to the grand Olympian eminence of High Romanticism."

"So do you feel differently about writing now? Has this Coleridgean bout with laudanum addiction changed your thinking? Do you want to be a High Romantic now, a Coleridge, a Byron? Or a 'modernist'?"

"I don't know. Maybe. But it's not working, so—"

"It's not working *yet*."

"Okay." Maiju looked at me and shrugged. "I don't know, J I. I just have no idea about any of this."

"But?"

"But I keep feeling this irresistible impulse to try."

"Good. Then you should keep trying."

"Yeah. And—"

"And?"

"And thanks, J I. Thanks for supporting me. Thanks for believing in me, despite the pain of these last months."

Now it was my turn to shrug.

"I love you, Maiju."

Ta nodded. "I love you too, J I. Always."

3

Did I dream this?

The revenant is in the Sörnäinen Slaughterhouse near the Fish Harbor. It is in line for the scales with twenty or thirty placid head of cattle. All along the line handlers make little adjustments with their electric prods, to keep the animals lined up neatly. The revenant too is occasionally zapped with one. It seems to be as placid as the other animals in line.

When the scrag reaches the scale, it steps onto it, and the pointer indicates the spring lies at rest—zero weight.

"Holy mackerel," the scale manager says, "do you even exist? You weigh nothing at all!"

"I exist," the revenant says archly. "Your scale must be broken."

"Hang on a second," the scale manager says. "Not so fast. Did I just imagine it, or did that pointer bob down into minus weight?"

"Impossible," the revenant says.

"Just for a split second. Try it again. Come on, Ostensible Oscar,[82] one more time. You zero it out, I agree, the scale's

---

[82] "Ostensible Oscar" here is an allusion to a Finnish children's rhyme: "Oskari Olematon, Nolla Katu Nolla" ("Oscar Ostensible, Zero Street Zero"—*olematon* is actually literally "nonexistent" or "nonbeing," but I've made it "ostensible" for the alliteration). There are hundreds of continuations of the rhyme—probably as many as kids who recite it—but most of them rhyme *luurankohissi* ("skeleton elevator") or *alaston missi* ("a naked

busted. But if you take it into minus weight, you're some kind of fucking demon."

The revenant sighs, steps off, steps on again.

"See? It did it again! Try it one more time!"

The revenant complies, but explains, and now it does definitely feel like a dream: "You know, what we take to be an object's weight is actually a conversion of the gravitational force it exerts, which is measured in newtons. At average gravity on this planet, a one-kilogram mass exerts a 9.8-newton force. Your average-sized apple exerts one newton of force. A smallish man like me should exert a force of around 490 to 500 newtons. Negative newtons are unbodies, not nu bodies."

Or this?

The revenant flies low through the night-time Helsinki streets. It seems to be heading toward Senate Square. The rain is siling down hard; the streets are flooding. This is unusual for February—this time of year it would usually be sleet or freezing rain—but not entirely unheard-of. It is late at night. The Lutheran cathedral on its hill of steps overlooking Senate Square is lit up; the strains of a large congregation singing "A Mighty Fortress is Our God" roll out as the entry doors open: a vesper service is just ending. The revenant hovers over the roof of the cathedral, this mighty Lutheran fortress, waiting for the parishioners to exit the church. The clouds continue to bucket water down all over the Square, but especially, it seems, on the steps outside the church. The parishioners begin to exit, raising umbrellas but still getting soaked as the gusty wind flips their umbrellas inside-out. When the revenant's eagle eye picks out its target, it swoops down out of the sky

---

beauty queen") with *Oskarin tissi* ("Oscar's tit"). A gender-bending after-life, tinged with the grotesque: a nice submerged invocation of this whole second "After" part of the novel—though of course only the Prologue and the Epilogue live at Zero Street Zero. [Tr.]

and gives a middle-aged man a rough shove down the famous 46 steps. The man tumbles treacherously; his neck snaps; his body comes to a stop with the glassy-eyed face in a deep puddle.

In the dream (if that is what this is) I know that the face in the puddle once belonged to Wolmar Henrik Ståhlberg. The man who pushed a live Algot Untola into the water has now been pushed into the water by a dead Algot Untola.

I hoped this one was just a dream:

At night while I'm asleep Maiju takes three bottles of laudanum out of ta's bag and stashes them in out-of-the-way places around the living room. Before sequestering the third bottle behind the books on one shelf, ta takes a deep pull on it.

2

Pretty sure this one wasn't a dream:

One night in mid-February of 1919 I was lying in bed in the dark, not yet asleep, not yet even sleepy, when I began to feel a telepathic presence. It was a body moving stealthily through the dark. I could dimly make out the outlines of a snowy city street.

Irmari? I guessed.

Yes. Who's this?

J I.

Hello, J I. Are you going to tag along?

I don't seem to have a choice in the matter, I thought.

Well, you're welcome to join me.

Where are you going?

You'll see.

In a few minutes ta turned into a cart entrance and proceeded to a door inside the courtyard. It was unlocked; Irmari opened it silently and stepped inside. The stairwell was dark, but I could feel ta climbing the stairs. On the second-floor landing ta moved to a wooden door on ta's right and jimmied the lock open with a knife. Ta proceeded through a dark entry hall and living room to a back bedroom. Under the covers on the double bed lay two dark lumps, presumably husband and wife, sleeping. Irmari stepped noiselessly to the head of the bed, then pounced with both arms: ta's right pinning the closer sleeper's torso to the mattress, ta's left covering the sleeper's mouth.

"Kyösti Wilkuna?" Irmari asked in a whisper.

The man nodded fearfully.

"You're going to die tonight."

Wilkuna's eyes went wide, and wild.

"Come outside with me."

Wilkuna shook his head vigorously, his eyes still wild.

"You're going to commit suicide," Irmari explained calmly, still in a whisper. "First you're going to write a note, then we're going to go outside and you're going to shoot yourself in the mouth with your own gun. You're going to do it because if you refuse, if you resist, if you cry out for help, I will shoot you and then your wife and children when they burst into the living room at sound of the gunshot. Now do you understand what's going to happen?"

Wilkuna didn't respond. His eyes flickered right and left.

"I believe you've suffered some mental health problems," Irmari said. "You have been contemplating suicide anyway. Now's your chance. No more dithering. All right?"

The spark seemed to go out of Wilkuna. He nodded.

And the rest of that incident went as planned. I watched Wilkuna take his pistol out from under his pillow, go into the living room to write the suicide note, then step outside, where he blew his brains out against the wall, and collapsed in a heap.[83]

Hope that wasn't too brutal for you, Irmari thought.

Wilkuna rejected a novel I wrote, I replied. *Maybe I wouldn't have gone to tonight's extreme to avenge that. But I expect you're acting on Algot's behalf, not mine.*

Exactly right.

---

[83] The author has taken poetic license here: Kyösti Wilkuna did commit suicide by shooting himself with his own gun, but almost four years later, not in February of 1919 but in December 1922, in Lapua, Ostrobothnia, nearly 400 km north of Helsinki. He was 43. His wife and children were in the house when he did it. [Tr.]

Next Irmari walked across town to another empty nighttime street, and stood waiting in an entranceway for a half hour or more. When a lone pedestrian turned onto the street and headed in his direction, Irmari took out a knife and flexed ta's right hand around the hilt. The pedestrian approached. Suddenly Irmari leaped out of hiding and plunged the knife into the other man—but ta's aim was a little off. The knife struck the right shoulder blade. The man yelped, and reacted quickly, lurching out of harm's way and running down the street. Irmari set off in pursuit, but just then two men came out of a doorway, saw what was happening, and seemed inclined to intervene, to protect the bleeding victim. Irmari, apparently deciding that discretion—or rather, getting the hell out of there—was the better part of valor, turned and ran the other direction.

Don't tell me, I thought. *Was that Eino Railo?*

None other.

So two assassinations in a single night. One successful, one thwarted. That's quite a piece of work.

I've got one more to go, Irmari thought.

What's the occasion?

What do you mean?

Well, I'm no expert, but my gut tells me that one assassination a night is probably a more workable solution.

I don't have that luxury, Irmari thought.

Luxury?

It all ends tomorrow.

What does? The world?

No. Irmari walked on.

What ends? I persisted.

You'll see.

The third intended victim was Senator Oswald Kairamo. Once Irmari had managed to sneak undetected through the darkened mansion into the senator's bedroom, however, he found it empty: the senator and his family were out. Frustrated, Irmari stabbed ta's bloody knife into the spot on the bed where the sleeping senator's heart would have been, and headed for the basement window through which ta had entered—and was attacked. A security guard? It was impossible to tell in the dark. Irmari fought back expertly, but the two were evenly matched. Each inflicted some damage, but not enough. Finally Irmari had had enough, and shoved ta's assailant hard over the back of a chair and fled through the front door. The guard pursued ta for a few blocks, but Irmari was apparently in better shape, and outdistanced the man handily.

1

When I woke the next morning I came out to the living room to find Maiju huddled under heavy blankets on the sofa, as usual—and a fire crackling away in the Dutch oven. I looked over at Maiju: did ta light the fire? But ta's head was turtled under the quilts. And of course we no longer had that wonderful telepathic connection.

I lit it, a familiar elderly male voice in my head said in Finnish.

Who's this? Why do I recognize that voice?

Never mind who I am. I just came to open Maiju up to your thoughts again, and you up to ta's. And it was chilly in the room, so I lit a fire. Hope that was all right.

Um, well, thanks. I mean, sure. Of course.

But who was it? Who had the power to open up our connection? Did anyone?

Then I saw him. It was of course pitch-black dark outside, and the only light in the room was cast by the flames in the oven, through the grate; but I could just make out a dim seated outline in a dark corner. The only detail I could see was that he was wearing spectacles: the yellow glow from the oven was reflected on them.

And then I remembered: that voice had come out of the blur by the window in Captain Sven Lille's basement apartment, just before the glasses had gone onto the blur's face with the candle's flame reflected in both lenses.

God? The Author of our fates?

J I, came Maiju's hesitant voice. *Who are you talking to?*

Maiju, I said, the emotion choking my thoughts. *You can hear me again! I have missed you so much!*

I've missed you too, J I. And I'm so glad we can talk again this way, because I have something I need to tell you.

But I knew, or at least I suspected, what it was.

No, Maiju, I pleaded. *Not that. Please, not that.*

I can't do this any more, J I. It's too hard.

Please don't do it, Maiju. I'm begging you. Stay with me.

When Algot comes to say goodbye, I'm going with him.

Ah, I thought. *That's what he meant.*

What's what who meant?

Irmari, I thought. *Last night. He said it all ends today. He meant it's time, didn't he? Algot's nine months of limbo are up. Irmari is going too. I suppose he arranged things so that he has to go.*

And indeed I could feel Irmari walking our way. Through ta's eyes I could see Algot on one side and M on the other.

I have to go too, Maiju thought, in the gentlest of voices.

Now but see, I thought, tears welling up inside me, *actually, in fact, you don't. You really don't. You don't owe him anything. He says he made you, he created all of us, but even if that's true, he's the one who got shot, not you. Not us. Stay.*

Please, J I, be strong.

No, you be strong! If you can just be strong enough to kick this habit, we can be together! Don't leave me!

I'm not that strong, J I. You were always the strong one. I've relied on you.

I've relied on you too! We've relied on each other!

Yes, I suppose we have. But it's too much now. If you love me, you'll let me go.

I was weeping now. Sobbing uncontrollably.

I do love you. I love you so much I never want to let you go!

Yes, I know you don't want to. *But you can. You're strong enough. You've suffered too, with me, these last months. It will be a relief for you too.*

I thought about that. I thought about it long enough for my sobs to subside. I blew my nose before resuming the conversation more calmly.

Maiju, I ventured, *yes, that time when Dead Algot was here talking about those English writers fighting the addiction for twenty or thirty years, I admit: I didn't want that. I did suffer with you. I suffered with your suffering body, because we didn't have this connection. It would have been sheer misery to limp along like that for decades more. But if you could* kick *the habit ...!*

I can't. I can't, J I. I'm sorry, but I'm too weak.

Okay, but Maiju, now we have our connection back! I'm in you again, and you're in me, and we're together again, in both bodies. As long as I can be with you, I won't suffer!

No, you won't, J I, because your body isn't in pain. Your body isn't addicted. Think about that.

Oh ... right ...

Besides, that person you were talking to when I woke up— he restored our connection to let us have this one last conversation together. Right?

Right, the elderly bespectacled man's voice said.

See? If I decided to stay, he would take it away again. Isn't that right as well?

Yes, the man's voice said.

I sank into myself, stymied. Thwarted.

You know, J I, Maiju thought. *You could come with us too.*

Come with you? How? What do you mean?

Just leave with us. Walk with us.

That's it? That's all that happens? You and Algot walk off together? And Irmari? And M?

And you too, if you choose.

Just walk off with you. Holding hands, the way we used to.
Yes.

I have to think about that.

Don't take too long. They're almost here.

I took a quick look and recognized the street. They were indeed almost here.

Did I want to walk off with that whole group? Was I ready to die?

There was one possibility that might make that tempting: *Would we be together for all eternity?*

I don't know.

Who does know? I turned to the man in the corner. *Do you know?*

No. Sorry.

At least we would be together walking to the Border, Maiju thought. *That would be something.*

But surely we can be together this way even if I don't walk with you, I thought. *Right, mister?*

Yes, he thought. *The connection will remain active till they cross the Border.*

I think, then—I couldn't believe I was mentally forming these terrifying words—*I think ... that I will stay.*

Okay, Maiju replied. *I'm glad. That means you're already letting me go.*

Yes, I suppose I am. I don't want to, but—*I'm imagining a life without you.*

That's good.

It's only half a life, but I'm realizing that half a life is better than none.

That feels to me like the right decision for you, J I.

I'm also imagining writing a memoir of you. Of our life together. A kind of immortality. For both of us.

I like the sound of that. What will you call it?

"*The Last Days of Maiju Lassila.*"

Just my last days? Not my whole life?

I haven't known you your whole life.

But how about "The Last Two and a Half Decades of Maiju Lassila"?

Kind of a mouthful.

True. Well, it's your book. You decide.

Maybe our connection will survive the Border crossing, and a year or two from now I can read it to you, and you can tell me what I got wrong.

Ha. J I, you always were a slow writer!

She thought it lovingly, of course. We laughed a little together. There were tears mixed in too.

And then—there came a knock on the door.

0

EPILOGUE

Once the Scraggy Pied Piper had led his three children—neither boys nor girls—across the Border into the Beyond, life calmed down considerably. There was no more of the revenge drama that the dead thing had been pursuing; no more of the drama of Maiju's struggle with addiction; no longer any threat of being discovered and arrested as Red agitators; and no M feeding us behind-the-scenes insights into political conspiracies and machinations. Life was ordinary ... mundane ... even boring. I was 43 years old, and could reasonably expect another three decades of that mundanity—possibly four. I wasn't sure I was up to it; but I set my mind to it. I cultivated a positive attitude. I was a post-war citizen of the twentieth century.

I missed Maiju terribly, at first. Of course. Ta's "death" left a gaping hole in my spirit that I thought would never be filled. We did maintain our telepathic connection as ta walked through the swirling spiritual landscape toward the shadowy Border—until it began to fade and break up. Then, nothing.

Fortunately, I had my work. I moved in with the baron, who liked to talk with me about theater and literature as I drove. My Russian improved rapidly. On the baron's Vironkatu property there was, in addition to his large house, a garage—a recently renovated former stables—with a coachman's apartment over it. That became my home—and is still my home today. It is quite comfortable; and I quite enjoy the driving. There's something about the engine puttering away, propelling us through the Helsinki streets, that seems like an entirely satisfying substitute for the excitement of those tumultuous nine months following the war. I have also learned to repair the car; and when the Ida Aalberg Theater failed after only a few months, I became the baron's full-time driver and mechanic. I considered applying for acting positions in other theaters, but I decided I didn't need any of that. I was happy being a driver and mechanic. From peasant to actor to novelist to actor to driver/mechanic. Not the most conventional career arc, I suppose; but somehow it felt like I had come full circle.

It was a bit of a humdrum life, maybe. When Maiju left it was like someone had snuffed out the fire in me, left me to gutter out in the dark. But I gradually began to realize that what was left was just—life. A humdrum life is still a life. There are worse things.

And there were bright moments. I didn't write any more novels, but I did write this memoir. It was, as you will fully appreciate, a labor of love. All those times I wept while living with Maiju made me weep again as I wrote about ta. All those times I blushed back then made me blush again as I wrote. I can't begin to tell you how deeply satisfying that was. Almost as if Maiju had come back to me—or never left.

After a month or two of toughing it out on my own, I went to the Stock Exchange Building to find the countess and her Clairvoyancy Parlour. I wanted to talk to Maiju. Unfortunately, the countess called for her in vain. There seemed to be no trace of Maiju in the afterlife. She tried M next, and then Irmari—no luck there either. She called up Algot, though, who said that Maiju, M, Irmari, and I were all what he called "second-order creatures" that could not be reached in the spirit world. It was as if Algot Untola's human "creations" were a house of cards that had fallen in on itself in death. I felt even more bereft, then. He had not only taken my Maiju; he had taken me.

To my surprise, when I came out through the red curtains I found Senator Oswald Kairamo in the hedge fund office. He wondered whether he had heard right, that I was looking for the spirits of Algot Untola, Maiju Lassila, and Irmari Rantamala. I took a chance and admitted that I was, hoping this admission would not lead to official suspicion falling upon me. And I'd guessed right. He wasn't interested in my interest; it was enough for him that all three were dead. So that was that.

I apologized that I had made him wait for the countess's services; but he smiled and said he wasn't waiting in line for a reading. He owned the place now. He had, he said, bought the place from his cousin, just before he died. A painter was coming over later that day to repaint the sign above the door The *Oswald* Kairamo Hedge Fund and Clairvoyancy Parlour. I congratulated him, wondering—but not asking—whether he was still allowing his clients to hedge their own deaths. Probably not, I guessed. Given that he was also a professional horticulturist, I figured he was probably sticking to—and profiting wildly off of—grain futures.

I later learned, too, that in 1919 he became chairman of the board at the National Bank. Did that make him fit to untie the mythical-hero literary-Areopagist shoelaces of Irmari Rantamala?

Behind my back, then, the countess harrumphed. The senator and I turned to her, and found her tapping the face of her watch and giving the senator a significant glower. The senator seemed to be about to protest, put his foot down—but then he sighed, turned to me, and said "If you'll excuse me?"

"Certainly," I said, as they vanished through the red curtains.

Selling the senator the hedge fund before it made for the Border, I thought, had been the revenant's last and best revenge.

A Note from the Head Manuscript Librarian at the National Library of Finland

(Written in English)

For legal purposes, my supervisor has asked me to confirm that Professor Douglas Robinson did visit our manuscript room, where he did read several manuscripts in the Algot Untola/Maiju Lassila collection, including the incomplete novels "Ville Sorsan romaani" ("Ville Sorsa's Novel") and "Veden haussa" ("Fetching Water"). We do not, however, possess a manuscript copy of a novel titled "Maiju Lassilan viimeiset päivät" ("The Last Days of Maiju Lassila"), and state emphatically and categorically that Professor Robinson cannot possibly have found it in our collection or read it in our reading room. I do not know whether that manuscript exists, nor does any other staff member at the National Library.

Signed,
Väinö Stenberg[84]
Head Manuscript Librarian
National Library of Finland

---

[84] It's probably just a coincidence, but Väinö Stenberg was another of Algot Untola's pseudonyms. [Tr.]

Legal, let's look into breaking this Robinson's contract with us. There's something fishy going on here. I'd rather not have our house dragged into anything untoward. [Ed.]

ABOUT ATMOSPHERE PRESS

Atmosphere Press is an independent, full-service publisher for excellent books in all genres and for all audiences. Learn more about what we do at atmospherepress.com.

We encourage you to check out some of Atmosphere's latest releases, which are available at Amazon.com and via order from your local bookstore:

ABOUT THE AUTHOR
AND TRANSLATOR

J.I. Vatanen was one of the heteronyms created by Algot Untola (1868-1918), a prolific Finnish novelist who achieved great popularity as his heteronym Maiju Lassila. Untola really was arrested, tried, and summarily executed as a Red agitator in May, 1918. It's doubtful Untola came back from the dead, or that Vatanen outlived his creator.

Douglas Robinson is a scholar and translator from Finnish who lives in Hong Kong and Shenzhen, PRC, and works at the Chinese University of Hong Kong, Shenzhen. He lived in Finland for 14 years in the 1970s and 1980s, and has translated novels by Finland's two greatest authors, Aleksis Kivi (1834-1872) and Volter Kilpi (1874-1939), and published scholarly studies of both.